Care

Personal Lives and Social Policy

Personal Lives and Social Policy
Series Editor: Janet Fink

This book forms part of a series published by The Policy Press in association with The Open University. The complete list of books in the series is as follows:

Sexualities: Personal Lives and Social Policy, edited by Jean Carabine
Care: Personal Lives and Social Policy, edited by Janet Fink
Work: Personal Lives and Social Policy, edited by Gerry Mooney
Citizenship: Personal Lives and Social Policy, edited by Gail Lewis

Notes on contributors to *Care: Personal Lives and Social Policy*

Janet Fink is a Lecturer in Social Policy in the Faculty of Social Sciences at The Open University. Her research interests are centred on the cultural turn in contemporary social policy and the intersections of family life and child welfare discourses during the second half of the twentieth century. Her recent publications include *Rethinking European Welfare* (co-edited with Gail Lewis and John Clarke) (Sage, 2001); 'Private lives, public issues: moral panics and the "family"' in *Journal for the Study of British Cultures* (2002); and 'Europe's cold shoulder: migration and the constraints of welfare in Fortress Europe' in *Soundings* (2002).

Katherine Holden is a Research Fellow at The University of the West of England. Her research interests are in the histories of singleness, the family and children in institutional care. Relevant publications are *The Family Story* (Longman, 1999), co-authored with Leonore Davidoff, Megan Doolittle and Janet Fink; 'Family, caring and unpaid work' in *Women in Twentieth Century Britain* (edited by Ina Zweiniger Bargielowska, Longman, 2001); and '"Nature takes no notice of morality": singleness, and *Married Love* in interwar Britain', *Women's History Review*, vol.8, no.3 (2002).

Barry Goldson is a Senior Lecturer at the Department of Sociology, Social Policy and Social Work Studies at The University of Liverpool. His teaching and research interests include the sociology of childhood and youth, criminology and criminal justice (particularly youth crime and youth justice), and state welfare policy. He has published widely in each of these areas and has six books, numerous contributions to books and journals, and many research reports to his name.

Yasmin Gunaratnam is a freelance consultant and Honorary Research Fellow at Southampton University. She has a particular interest in issues of 'race' and gender in health and social care. Her PhD research was an ethnographic study of the production of 'race' and ethnicity in a London hospice that developed from her personal experiences of caring for her mother through a terminal illness. Yasmin has also done research on minoritized carers and on 'race', gender and professional identity among mental health nurses.

Personal Lives and Social Policy

Edited by Janet Fink

This publication forms part of the Open University course DD305 *Personal Lives and Social Policy*. Details of this and other Open University courses can be obtained from the Course Information and Advice Centre, PO Box 724, The Open University, Milton Keynes MK7 6ZS, United Kingdom: tel. +44 (0)1908 653231; e-mail general-enquiries@open.ac.uk. Alternatively, you may visit the Open University website at http://www.open.ac.uk where you can learn more about the wide range of courses and packs offered at all levels by The Open University.

To purchase a selection of Open University course materials visit the webshop at www.ouw.co.uk, or contact Open University Worldwide, Michael Young Building, Walton Hall, Milton Keynes MK7 6AA, United Kingdom, for a brochure: tel. +44 (0)1908 858785; fax +44 (0)1908 858787; e-mail ouwenq@open.ac.uk

First published 2004 by The Policy Press in association with The Open University

The Open University
Walton Hall
Milton Keynes
MK7 6AA
United Kingdom
www.open.ac.uk

The Policy Press
Fourth Floor, Beacon House
Clifton
Bristol
BS8 1QU
United Kingdom
www.policypress.org.uk

The opinions expressed are not necessarily those of the Course Team or of The Open University.

British Library Cataloguing-in-Publication Data
A catalogue record for this book is available from the British Library.

Library of Congress Cataloguing-in-Publication Data
A catalogue record for this book has been requested.

Edited, designed and typeset by The Open University.

Printed and bound in Great Britain by The Bath Press, CPI Group.

ISBN 1 86134 519 4

1.1

Contents

Preface

Care: Personal Lives and Social Policy is the second of four books in a new series published by The Policy Press in association with The Open University. The series takes an interdisciplinary and theoretically informed approach to the study of social policy in order to examine the ways in which the two domains of *personal lives* and *social policy and welfare practice* are each partially shaped and given meaning by the other. This process of mutual constitution is explored in the books through core practices of the everyday. Such an approach is both exciting and innovative. It is also indicative of a growing recognition within the social sciences that 'the personal' is a valuable lens of analysis. More generally, the series is concerned not only with debates and questions that are highly visible in social policy, but also with those that tend to be marginalized or silenced and how these might be interpreted through the use of different theoretical perspectives, conceptual tools and research evidence. Overall, therefore, the books move beyond what are usually considered to be the parameters of social policy and its study.

The four books make up the core texts of an Open University course entitled *Personal Lives and Social Policy*. The first book, *Sexualities: Personal Lives and Social Policy*, considers why questions of sex and sexuality matter for the study of social policy and, in turn, illustrates how such questions provide important insights into the relationship between personal lives and social policy. Its concerns with the normative and taken-for-granted assumptions about sexuality, that inform social policy and welfare practices, establish the central interest of the series – the dynamics by which social policy and personal lives intersect and become entangled.

This second book, *Care: Personal Lives and Social Policy*, focuses on the meanings and definitions attributed to care and examines the norms and values associated with care relationships that are embedded in welfare policy and practice. The book illustrates the highly charged and often contradictory nature of care relations by exploring issues of power, conflict and control and considering the different spaces and places where questions about care have been lived out, debated and struggled over.

The third book, *Work: Personal Lives and Social Policy*, traces the central place that work has been afforded, historically, in policy-making and the extent to which it has remained an unproblematic category not only for policy-makers but also in the study of social policy. The book foregrounds the contingent relationship between work and welfare in order to examine the ways in which this arena of policy practices and discourses has developed around particular constructions of personal lives.

The fourth and final book, *Citizenship: Personal Lives and Social Policy*, looks at ideas and meanings associated with citizenship in order to broaden and problematize the term. In particular, it emphasizes the importance of moving away from associating citizenship with rights and obligations within nation-states towards recognizing how a consideration of multiple belongings and practices of the everyday opens up the study of social policy to new and challenging questions.

Although these books are edited volumes, each chapter has been specially written to contribute not only to the exploration of the mutual constitution of personal lives and social policy, but also to the process of student learning. The books have, therefore, been constructed as interactive teaching texts which encourage engagement with and further reflection on the themes, issues and arguments presented in the chapters. The process of interaction is organized around:

- *activities* – variously made up of exercises, tasks and questions, highlighted in colour, which have been designed to extend or consolidate understanding of particular aspects of the chapters;

- *comments* – interpretations and discussions of the activities, which provide opportunities for readers to compare their own responses with those of the author(s);

- *in-text questions* – short questions, again in colour, that build into the chapter opportunities for consideration of core points or arguments;

- *key words* – terms and concepts, highlighted in colour in the text and in the margins, which are central to the arguments, theoretical perspectives and research questions being used and interrogated by the author(s).

In addition, the opening chapter of each book has been written to provide a critical introduction to key issues, ideas, theories and concepts associated with the book's field of interest. The individual books are self-contained but there are references to other chapters and other books in the series. Such references help readers not only to make connections between the books, but also to understand and reflect on the themes and debates that run across the series overall.

The series has been shaped and informed by discussions within the Open University Course Team. Each member of the Team brought to these discussions their own interests, enthusiasms and fields of expertise, but never lost sight of the overall aims of the series and their commitment to those aims. The series is, therefore, the product of a genuinely interdisciplinary and collaborative process. This also means that contributions have been made to all the chapters of the books within this series by people who are not explicitly named as authors. The process of collaboration extends further, however, than the production of materials by academics. In writing chapters, the Course Team and consultant authors have been advised and guided by an external assessor, a tutor panel and a developmental testing panel. The wide-ranging involvement and assistance from the editors, designers and picture researchers have been invaluable in the production of these accessible and attractive texts. Course managers have used their knowledge and skills to resolve the many questions and difficulties that arose during the course's development. Secretaries brought their expertise to the styling and organization of seemingly endless manuscript drafts – and did so with admirable good humour. We thank them all for their work and support which are reflected throughout this book, the series and the course as a whole.

Janet Fink

CHAPTER I

Questions of Care

by Janet Fink

Contents

1   Introduction

Every day we encounter the very different meanings, practices and relations of care as Figure 1.1 illustrates. Soap operas and the problem pages of magazines and newspapers invite us to explore the difficulties of providing care for those we love. Features in magazines and guest appearances on television chat shows encourage personal confessions about the nature of the most intimate aspects of caring relationships with children, lovers, parents and spouses. In the UK we are exhorted through charity events such as Comic Relief and Children in Need to donate money as an expression of our care for those who have needs that are not being met by other statutory and charitable programmes of aid. And television documentaries and newspaper articles regularly feature 'crises' in care provision for disabled and older people, and highlight the neglect and abuse experienced by children in the care system.

Figure 1.1   Encounters with care in the media

At an individual level, our care relations construct a range of the social connections we experience across generations and between sexes, in households and neighbourhoods, in the workplace and within welfare institutions themselves (Hoggett, 2000). Our encounters with 'normal' life transitions of birth and death bring into stark relief questions about the giving and receiving of care and the emotions that surround these exchanges. We are involved daily in negotiating and juggling our care relationships with friends, lovers, neighbours, work colleagues and family members, which we may welcome, appreciate, take for granted or resent. For those involved in paid care work, the boundaries of these relationships and the emotions that are provoked are even more complex because they overlap with assumptions about the care needs of clients and patients.

In terms of policy, care has become a key concern and an expanding research area because of shifting demographic, economic and cultural factors; an ageing population, the growing numbers of women in paid work and a perceived fragmentation of family life, can be expected to have profound effects on the future demand for and supply of care. These changes and their implications are the focus of ideological debates about individual and state responsibility for the provision of care. Caring is increasingly recognized as an expression of citizenship obligation in New Labour debates about the meaning of citizenship and the nature of its responsibilities and obligations (Harris, 2002; **Lewis, 2004**). Moreover, the state is regularly engaged with the definition and meaning of care, attempting to curb the perceived escalation in its costs while, at the same time, developing strategies to ensure its safe and effective delivery (Williams, 2001).

With this range and intensity of focus it should not be surprising that efforts to understand and regulate the meanings and practices of care can be the subject of conflict, not only in policy-making but also in our everyday lives. One of the reasons for this is that care, like sexuality (**Carabine, 2004**), is understood to be at the core of the most intimate and personal aspects of our lives, and to inform what is considered to be 'natural' and 'normal' in our relationships with others. As a result, many of our caring relationships and obligations are assumed to develop out of 'normal' heterosexual practices. It is popularly taken for granted that the nuclear family is a key site of care, where love and nurture are always available alongside more practical forms of support. Similarly, everyday encounters with professionals such as nurses, doctors, teachers and social workers are charged with deep-rooted expectations that a 'normal' part of their role and responsibilities is the delivery of care alongside treatment, education or advice.

At the core of this book, therefore, is a determination to interrogate the ways in which our personal lives and social policies have embedded within them normative assumptions not only about who should provide care, but also how and where that care should take place.

Aims   With this in mind, the aims of the book are:

- To explore how personal experiences of care reinforce or confound the concepts and meanings of care that are located in the domain of social policy and society more generally.

- To investigate how care relations are politically, socially and culturally shaped and the effects of this upon social policy and the personal lives of those providing and receiving care.

- To consider the different contexts of care and question how experiences and ways of practising care are shaped by perceived, but unstable, boundaries between work and home, masculine and feminine, paid and unpaid, 'the public' and 'the personal'.

This book is engaged with interrogating ideas and ideals associated with care together with their influences in the mutual constitution of personal lives and social policy. We have chosen three topics to explore the complex and multi-layered nature of these associations. These are: single women's caring identities; the care and control of children in secure accommodation and young offender institutions; and the racialized relations of care in the hospice setting. Each highlights the significance that age, class, gender, 'race' and sexuality plays in the analysis of care relations. The authors use qualitative research evidence and different theoretical perspectives to explore the tensions generated through the intersections of these social divisions. Together, these chapters illustrate the extent to which care is a constant feature in understanding our sense of self and the nature of our relations with others. At the same time, they highlight the ways in which welfare discourses and practices shape these relationships and give or deny them meaning and validity.

This introductory chapter provides the framework through which to locate the discussions and arguments that are played out in the rest of the book. It has three main sections which take you through:

- the different ways in which care, caring and carers can be understood;

- how feminist and psychoanalytic theory have been used to explore the meanings and practices of care; and

- the shifting nature of policy and the different forms of its intervention in the domain of care.

It brings into focus the different spaces and places where questions about care in all its dimensions have been lived out, debated and struggled over. It does not offer any easy answers to these questions, but rather suggests conceptual and analytic tools that may be helpful in exploring this 'normal' yet deeply ambiguous topic and the complex nature of its connections to our personal lives and the making of social policy.

2   Conceptualizing care, caring and carers: assumptions and contradictions

There are many elements to our understanding of care, caring and carers and this section introduces some of the diverse ways in which these concepts have been conceptualized and, thereby, highlights the slippery, ambiguous and contested nature of the terms associated with care relations. But first, Activity 1.1 will help you to identify some of the stereotypical images of caring that saturate popular culture.

ACTIVITY 1.1

Take a little time to think about the representations of care and carers you have recently encountered either in magazines, newspapers and novels, or on television and radio.

- What roles were predominantly given to women?
- How do questions of age, class, disability and 'race' inform the representations?
- Do these representations disrupt what might be seen as 'traditional' attitudes towards women, family life and care?
- How might changes in the labour market help explain such disruptions?
- Are your experiences of care reflected in these media images?

COMMENT

As your analysis of the images of care in the UK today may have demonstrated, there are many connections between ideas about femininity, family life and the domestic domain. So, for example, representations of carers tend to focus on women who are at home, not in a public place, and who provide care in natural, effortless and generous ways (Hochschild, 1995). Contemporary advertisements for household appliances continue to portray 'the woman-in-the-house' as taking on the main tasks and responsibilities for care (Silva, 1999). Other sets of images inform and are informed by the changes in the employment market and the growth in women's employment (**Mooney, 2004b**). Much television advertising, for instance, portrays women at the beginning or end of their paid work as they dispatch children to school or prepare the evening meal. There are also many documentaries and television series which feature the 'caring' professions.

informal
formal

Care, therefore, can be understood as **informal** (unpaid) or **formal** (paid). It can mean nurture or treatment. It can refer to the protection of children 'in care' or 'the duty of care' expected of schools. It is used to indicate private or state accommodation for disabled people and 'elderly' disoriented people. Care can also mean imprisonment in secure hospitals (James, 1992). Such meanings tend to suggest the different spaces and places of care where the experiences and ways of practising care can be traced. These spaces, places, experiences and practices also give meaning to the concept of 'carer'. On the one hand carers can be paid workers in the 'public' sphere or, on the other, they might be unpaid volunteers, friends, family members, lovers or neighbours providing care in the domestic domain. They can be 'romanticized' or represented as 'victims' in the media and academic research (Gunaratnam, 1993). But wherever carers are located and in whatever ways they identify themselves as carers, their personal lives will be shaped and negotiated through the gendered, aged and racialized assumptions about care and its provision as we explore shortly.

2.1   Doing care and being caring

First we want to highlight the complexities and ambiguities embedded within the concept of care itself. Hilary Graham (1983, p.13) suggests that it is essential to make the distinction between 'what caring means and what caring entails', so that we can disentangle those meanings of care which denote caring for and those that suggest caring about. To put it another way, it is important in reflecting upon the meanings of care and caring to distinguish between 'doing' and 'being'. This is a distinction which has been made by Joan Tronto (1993) who argues that care should be seen as an activity (doing care) and a disposition (being caring).

ACTIVITY 1.2

Read Extract 1.1 from *The Family Life of Old People* (1957).

- How many different examples of care can you trace in this diary excerpt?
- Can you distinguish between the performances of care as an activity and a disposition?

Extract 1.1   'The family life of old people'

Mrs Tucker, 16 Bantam Street, aged sixty, living with infirm husband in terraced cottage.

Monday

7.45 a.m. I got up, went down, and put my kettle on the gas – half-way – then I raked my fire out and laid it, swept my ashes up, and then cleaned my hearth. Then I set light to my fire, then sat down for a while, then I made tea and me and Dad had a cup.

9.20 a.m. I went out for the Daily Mirror and fags for Dad. About eight people said 'Good Morning' with a nice smile, then I replied back. Then I went home and prepared oats and bread, butter and tea and me and Dad sat for breakfast. When we finished I cleared away and swept and mopped my kitchen out.

11.15 a.m. I started to get dinner on, then Mrs Rice, a neighbour, asked me to get her coals in, and she will take my bag-wash, also get my dog's meat. We had a nice chat about Mother's Day. I showed her my flowers and card which Alice sent. It was very touching, a box of chocs from John, stockings and card from Rose, card and 5s. from Bill, as I know they all think dearly of me.

1 p.m. My daughter Alice came with baby. We had dinner together.

2 p.m. My daughter Rose and husband came. I made them a cup of tea and cake.

3.15 p.m. Dad and I sat to listen to radio.

5 p.m. We both had tea, bread and cheese Dad, bread and jam myself. When finished I cleared away again.

> 7 p.m. My son John and his wife called to see if we were all right before they went home from work.
>
> 8 p.m. I did a little mending.
>
> 10 p.m. We went to bed.
>
> (Townsend, 1957, pp.296–7)

COMMENT

As Extract 1.1 illustrates, it can at times be difficult to disentangle the ways in which caring about and caring for someone overlap in our personal lives. Mrs Tucker is engaged throughout the day in *doing* care as she shops and prepares food for her family but, at the same time, these are also activities in which she might understand herself as *being* caring. Similarly, the visits by her son and daughters and their presents to her on Mother's Day can be regarded as expressions of being caring and doing care. It is evident too that the relationship between Mrs Tucker and her neighbour is one of mutual care and support, but again it is difficult to distinguish activity and disposition. What is significant is the extent to which Mrs Tucker's portrayal of her daily life reflects and reinforces expectations about the ways in which relations between wives and husbands, parents and children, and those with friends and neighbours, are lived out through physical and emotional expressions of care.

The detailing by Mrs Tucker of her day carries little suggestion that she makes any distinction between caring about and caring for those closest to her. Yet we should not presume that intimate relationships in which people care *about* each other equal an ability or willingness to care *for* them. The physically intimate tasks and activities that are necessary in some forms of caring can evoke feelings of embarrassment, distaste or hostility even where those concerned care about each other. Personal care might involve touching, nakedness or contact with excreta which, as Clare Ungerson (1983, 1987) has argued, can pose problems for those caring relationships in which the boundaries of taboo and social constraint are perceived as being breached. Therefore, questions of gender and age, together with the nature of the personal relationship in which care is required or expected, raise difficult issues. For example, a mother may be able to accept performing particular tasks for an adult male son that may not be acceptable in reverse (Twigg and Atkin, 1994). A father may be reluctant to provide physical care for a daughter when she reaches puberty. And the sexual and emotional intimacy experienced by spouses and partners may not easily equate into the physical intimacy demanded by some care relationships.

Care, as activity, can therefore be demanding and alien for both the carer and the recipient of such care. It may not fit easily within the normative framework through which care provided by family members, but especially mothers and daughters, tends to be conceptualized. Care practices can evoke intense physical, emotional and psychological responses which, in turn, can have profound effects upon our sense of self or 'who we are'. Such responses clearly have implications for the definition and regulation of caring relationships at the individual and institutional level as we explore through the chapters of this book.

These chapters usefully illustrate the highly charged and often contradictory nature of our responses to care relations and tease out those issues of conflict, power and control that are often embedded in them. For example, Chapter 2 considers the complex narratives deployed by single women to explain and make sense of the ways in which *demands* for care from family members, as well as their own *desires* to care, impacted upon their personal lives in inter-war England. Personal accounts are also drawn upon in Chapter 4 where they are again used to unpick another strand in the complex web of care practices and relationships that is the concern of this book. Through a discussion of inter-cultural care within one hospice, which makes simultaneous connections to other broader experiences and social spaces, Yasmin Gunaratnam explores the nature of identifications and power relations in the health services and the ways in which these inform and shape the racialization of care. The question of power in analyses of care is considered in Chapter 3. Here Barry Goldson critically examines the meanings of care to explore how power is exercised over those children who are understood by the state to require care, protection and direction. This approach highlights that ideas about caring for children cannot be easily separated from questions of their control.

2.2   Identifying carers

The multi-layered meanings that are clustered within the concept of care should alert us to the difficulties that might be encountered in defining 'carer'. As a concept it has a relatively short history, in that whether carer is taken to refer to a personal identity, a welfare subject or a category of people, it is unlikely that individuals readily identified with it before the 1980s. It was not until this point that the role of the informal carer became visible as a result of both feminist research into the issue of women's caring responsibilities (as we see in section 3) and the increasingly powerful lobbying voice of the Carers National Association (CNA). Moreover, the term 'carer' is not just historically specific, it is also culturally specific. In many Asian languages, for example, there is no precise equivalent word for carer: 'I think that it is difficult for us Asian people to see ourselves as "carers" ... the idea is not something that is part of our culture or language, it is just another part of family life' (quoted in Gunaratnam, 1991, p.2).

For these reasons Bill Bytheway and Julia Johnson (1998, p.241) have argued that 'we can think of the concept of "carer" as a social construction, a category created through the interplay between individual experience and various interest groups – policy-makers, researchers and pressure groups'.

The category of carer – as opposed to the actual emotional and physical experiences of doing care and being caring – has come to have particularly narrow connotations in that it tends to refer to unpaid, inter-generational care by women, for example between mothers and young children or adult daughters and parents. These connotations have not been left unchallenged. Research into care relations and the life course has pointed to the responsibilities undertaken by both children and older spouses in the provision of informal care.

Investigations into the phenomenon of young carers have demonstrated the extent of care work among children and young people and its effects upon their personal lives. Although the numbers of children providing substantial or regular care are not large, Figure 1.2 illustrates the degree to which care needs might impact upon children.

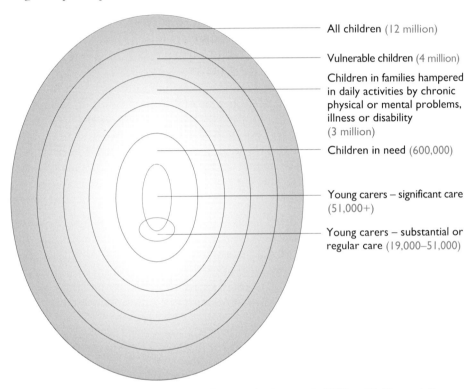

Figure 1.2   Children's labour of love (Source: Becker et al., 2001, p.76, Figure 6.1)

Young carers' experiences of care work challenge assumptions about the meaning of childhood in that their lives can be framed by partial or complete responsibility for the emotional and physical care of adults. Such experiences subvert normative ideas about childhood as a period of dependency, although there is no suggestion that young carers and their parents do not have mutually supportive and loving relationships, as we discuss later. Nevertheless, the personal lives of young carers are shaped by their material and intimate experiences of family life and, in this, social policy can be understood to play a central role. For instance, the educational and material circumstances of young carers' lives can be constrained because disability and illness within families often results in a reliance on state benefits for prolonged periods of time. Moreover, the needs of young carers for physical, emotional or material support are seldom comprehensively met, because although local authorities have a duty to recognize and assess their needs, there is no obligation to provide services to them (Becker et al., 2001). The very particular characteristics of young people's experiences of providing care, and their own characteristics of young people's experiences of providing care, and their own individual needs, bring into sharp focus the different meanings and effects of informal care within family relationships.

There is also evidence that care between spouses in older age also disrupts any easy conceptualization of carer as a category. Sara Arber and Jay Ginn (1990), for example, have illustrated that four in ten carers are spouses, mainly 'elderly', and half of these are men. Such statistics disrupt the prevailing view that older people are axiomatically care receivers and highlight the extent to which providing care is a regular feature of the majority of older people's personal lives (**Widdowson, 2004**). Louise Ackers and Peter Dwyer (2002) have pursued these issues further. Their research into retirement migration in the European Union (EU) covers a range of issues but, for our purposes, it highlights very well the extent of inter-generational support that takes place within the retired population. Through interviews with retired migrants, Ackers and Dwyer challenge the stereotypical perception of retirement as a period of passivity and dependency in terms of care. Their analysis demonstrates the extent to which the conceptualization of carer fails to grasp the ever shifting inter-generational caring responsibilities of older people, which are carried out in support of not only their own 'more aged parents', but also their children and grandchildren.

Conceptualizing carers means, therefore, being sensitive to questions of age and gender. Acknowledging the significant role that men play in providing care in older age can also bring into view other occupations and professions in which men take up caring positions. Recognition of, for example, male nurses or male care assistants can usefully challenge conceptions about care as well as gendered assumptions that it is women who are 'natural' carers.

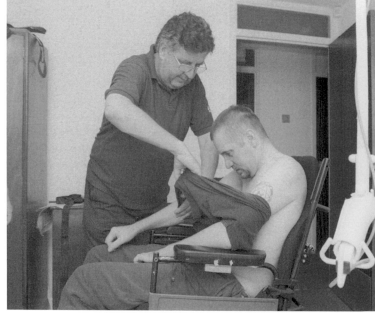

Figure 1.3   Male care workers

However, this is a two-way process and we should recognize that the effects of these assumptions upon the personal lives of male care workers can be profound. In particular, care work by men raises issues of self-esteem, status and sexuality, rarely considered in the context of female carers, but which can organize the work practices of these men and the relationships with their clients.

ACTIVITY 1.3

Read Extract 1.2 which describes the experiences of three male care workers who formed part of an empirical study of help with washing and bathing provided for older and disabled people living at home (Twigg, 2000).

- How are 'natural' and 'normal' assumptions about care provision constraining opportunities for the male carers to make intimate and emotional connections to their clients?
- How might such constraints impact upon the ways in which these men understand themselves as carers and as caring?

Extract 1.2   Men and care work

A male care worker going into a female client's home was perceived as problematic ... Interchanges in a private home have a different quality to them; they are by their nature more intimate. Concern about male care workers also reflects more general anxieties about males in the care sector. The exposure of the extent of sexual abuse of children and vulnerable adults in care homes has resulted in a situation where all male workers are to some degree under suspicion. Male care workers have to be careful and this reinforces a 'professional approach'.

All three men were aware of an undercurrent around the issue of their sexuality. They were all heterosexual, but men who work in caring occupations suffer from a series of cultural assumptions that since this is women's work, men who do it must be effeminate and therefore gay ... They also suffer from the homophobia of male clients, or at least from male anxieties about intimate tending by another man. Hegemonic masculinity in the West is constructed around the rejection of the homosexual ... Men share ideas of other men as sexually predatory, and assuring oneself that the care worker is not a homosexual was important for some clients.

(Twigg, 2000, p.130)

The gendered stereotypes of women as 'natural' carers and men as 'natural' sexual predators (**Carabine, 2004**) shape the personal lives of men employed in the care sector. They necessitate the construction of what are understood to be clear boundaries between 'the personal' and 'the professional' so that the more physically intimate care practices can be delivered with as little tension as possible for both client and carer. Doing what is perceived to be 'women's work' is therefore not without its costs to men's understanding of themselves, both as caring individuals and as professional carers. This is typically resolved by men accepting positions and responsibilities that take them away from the 'front line of care' and establishing themselves in more managerial aspects of care work where their masculinity is reinforced and not challenged (Twigg, 2000).

So far our emphasis has been on how a specific focus on age and gender can throw valuable light on the conceptualization of the term 'carer'. The question of 'race' and its intersections with these social divisions is also deeply significant. For example, the personal lives of Asian and African-Caribbean carers, reveal how their experiences of unpaid care-giving are supported or constrained by welfare discourses and practices. From the research evidence available, which is not extensive, it is clear that, for all carers, there are common features in the physical, emotional and financial consequences of care-giving. But the emotional consequences for Asian and African-Caribbean carers may be exacerbated by welfare practice and provision with its assumptions about cultural practices and the racist attitudes of some service providers. In addition, informal carers from racialized minorities experience greater material hardship because of racial inequalities in income, employment and housing (Atkin and Rollings, 1996).

The personal lives of paid care workers from racialized minorities are also shaped and constrained by the nature of racism in welfare services and society more generally which can mean that:

> black ethnic minority people are more often employed in areas like mental disability or psychogeriatrics where they are required to control and discipline clients. Black ethnic minority workers are thus differentially positioned in the harsher and more punitive parts of the welfare system dealing with the least powerful clients.
>
> (Twigg, 2000, p.195)

Considerations of racism and the social division of 'race' bring new dimensions to the questions of choices, control and power that we pointed to earlier. However, one of the important (but largely missing) areas in this field is the issue of 'whiteness'. In much research and policy analysis, caring among white families has been a consistent focus and topic of interest. There has been far less interest in the ways in which 'white' as a racialized identity is understood or how 'white' carers understand themselves. Yet, an awareness of the complexity of racialized identities can help us appreciate the different ways in which carers can be positioned in formal and informal care relations, and the effects of those differences upon their personal lives.

2.3   The dynamics of care relationships

Despite the difficulties of incorporating the range and diversity of care experiences within the category of carer, the Carers National Association (CNA) has actively sought to identify carers' needs and to have them acknowledged in policy and legislation. These needs include: recognition of the quantity and quality of carers' unpaid care work; services tailored to individual circumstance; opportunities for a break; and information on benefits and services (Barnes, 1997). The CNA is a powerful lobby and it has been influential in the development and implementation of, for example, the Carers (Recognition and Services) Act of 1995 and the policy package 'Caring about Carers: A National Strategy for Carers' (1999). In addition, the Labour Government and its model of citizenship, based on active participation and self-reliance, seeks to recognize the contribution that informal carers make on behalf of the state.

However, there have been concerns expressed about the implications of such recognition in policy-making. The political shift, which emphasizes the rights of carers in discourses of citizenship and in recent social policy, tends to neglect the effects upon the social and personal identity of those receiving care. That is, the emphasis upon carers as a resource and an asset to society suggests that those people receiving care are not of equal value (Harris, 2002). We should acknowledge, therefore, that the sustained focus upon carers can serve to reinforce ideas that care is a simple one-way process. This can result in the cared-for person being constituted as passive and a dependent 'burden' upon the carer, which closes down opportunities to acknowledge 'the multiplicity and reciprocal nature of many caring relationships' (Bytheway and Johnson, 1998, p.242). It also suggests that there is a 'primary carer' who is easily identifiable and in control of the caring relationship.

The greatest challenge to the concept of 'carer' and its recent emphasis in social policy and practice guidelines has come from the independent living movement, which represents the views and interests of some groups of disabled people. Its critique of feminist theories of care, with their emphasis on the responsibilities of women as informal carers, is considered in some detail later. Here, our concern is with the extent to which the experiences and views of the carer appear to have been given precedence in policy-making over the perspectives of those who are cared for as summarized by Liz Lloyd:

> [Caring About Carers: A National Strategy for Carers] does pay lip-service to disabled people's groups and to the need to 'balance' the rights of both people in the caring relationships. However, there is little evidence in the strategy of the perspectives of the people who are cared for and in this respect it can be seen as divisive. Indeed, it runs the real risk of putting the interests of carers above those of the people who are on the receiving end of care. For example, the consultative conference held in November 1998 was addressed by a wide range of speakers, but none that represented the interests or perspectives of disabled people. In privileging the views of carers' organizations, the government has failed to grasp an opportunity to develop more inclusive and creative ideas about the nature of care and support.
>
> (Lloyd, 2000, pp.148–9)

There is often also an absence of the perspectives of disabled people in the research literature on care, which rarely includes narratives of their personal experiences. Such narratives, as this book as a whole emphasizes, are especially valuable to our understanding of the complex dynamics of care relationships. The wide failure, therefore, to incorporate evidence about the personal lives of disabled people into analyses of care practices and relations has had several effects. First, it has perpetuated the continuing tendency of discourses of care to constitute disabled people as an inevitable burden on their families, thereby setting up a dichotomy between 'normal' families and families with disabled members. This suggests that one set of relationships is benign and 'the other is problematic and pathological' (Shakespeare, 2000, p.55). Second, it has elided the ways in which care relationships can be

reciprocity
interdependence

understood as being built around elements of **reciprocity** and **interdependence**, failing, thereby, to acknowledge that in some places and at some times, we have all experienced giving and receiving care (Williams, 2001). Finally, the relative absence of personal narratives about the experiences of being cared-for means that the call from disabled people for

independence

independence through the expansion of personal assistance schemes has received too little attention (**Shildrick, 2004**).

ACTIVITY 1.4

Take a moment to read Extract 1.3 from a report into the care of disabled people with 'high support needs'.

- How is the need and desire for independence being expressed?
- Why is the notion of independence important for thinking about how the personal lives of disabled people are shaped by welfare provision?

Extract 1.3　Pat

Just recently I had a reassessment of my care package and the social worker was quite worried that I might be putting myself at risk by getting into bed at the end of the day on my own, because I do have osteoporosis as well as multiple sclerosis. But I like my independence and the thought of having someone watching the same television programmes that you are watching, just hovering around for the time you need to go to the toilet, or the time you want to go to bed ... She wanted to increase my hours into the evening, but it was important for me to keep a little bit of my own real independence, the fact that I'm on my own and that's what I want ...

...

I wanted help to do the shopping, but home care workers won't come *with* you to do the shopping. They will do the shopping *for* you, which seems absolutely stupid because you can't have any involvement in what's being bought for you. People think I'm nuts but I like going shopping because I can feel the vegetables and the fruit. It's about choice again. You don't always know in advance what you want do you (emphasis added).

(Kestenbaum, 1999, pp.31–3)

COMMENT

The excerpts in Extract 1.3 illustrate the different ways in which Pat understands her independence – as a desire to be alone, to have choices and to be involved in everyday taken-for-granted activities. The delivery of personal care needs is, therefore, complex and the subject of negotiation between carers and individuals receiving care as they establish the boundaries between support, enablement, intrusion and control.

The use of the term 'carer' in discussions of care relations needs careful thought and attention. Our brief analysis has suggested that the intersections of age, gender and 'race' disrupt any notion of a coherent category of carers with similar experiences, identifications and subject positions. The needs, desires and expectations of people considered to require care, for whatever reason, are equally diverse and complex, thus, even further unsettling definitions of 'the carer' and assumptions about the experiences of receiving care. Moreover, the delivery and receipt of care, whether paid or unpaid, is a dynamic process in which the lives of both parties are woven together, disrupting any simplistic division between dependence and independence. The emphasis on the carer's role in recent policy-making has not taken into account the diverse ways in which care relationships are negotiated between the carer and the individual receiving care, nor does it take into account the interdependence of those relationships. The result is that too few of the complexities of care and caring in our personal lives have been acknowledged or addressed in social policy.

2.4   New (and old) caring arenas

The final strand in our discussion of the conceptualization of care, caring and carers moves on to the growing divide between those who are constituted as having responsibilities to care and those who are paid to take on those responsibilities. This is an area of intense negotiation between women, and between women and men, in contemporary Western society as the professional middle classes increasingly seek to resolve the work–life balance by the use of paid carers (**Mooney, 2004b**).

While caring as disposition remains central to our understanding of the meanings of our intimate and familial relationships, in recent years caring as activity might be seen as increasingly separated from those relationships. There has, for example, been a significant growth in the paid employment of women within households to provide care for babies and children, do housework and give practical and nursing assistance to older and disabled people. There has been a similar rise in people, predominantly women, working for pay in other sites of care such as nurseries, after-school clubs, residential homes and nursing homes. This work is invariably low paid, low status, insecure, with few career opportunities as well as being demanding, both physically and emotionally. This can result in significant pressures upon care staff and situations of inadequate and, at times, abusive treatment of children, and disabled and older people.

Hierarchies of age, class, 'race' and ethnicity allow some women opportunities to reduce the tasks and activities of care but, as Extract 1.4 illustrates, they can aggravate or increase the responsibilities of other women. This is taken from

Figure 1.4   Care as headline news

an interview with Mrs H who migrated from Jamaica in the early 1960s to join her husband and who left one daughter with her mother.

Extract 1.4   Mrs H
Sometimes we would eat less or buy the cheapest thing to send for them home ... We had a hard time over here making it, but I determined that since I'm here already ... I make a parcel and post it. That's why they [the family] believe we are so rich over here, because we would deny ourselves to always care for them there ... I sent for my big daughter, and when she came she was alright because she had me to come to and she was well catered for. She went to a good school. I sent her to a church school. I do overtime at the children's hospital. I go in early at five o'clock. I start work at six, cleaning ... And when I finish at three o'clock, I might run home, jump on a bus and run, and get something for my daughter coming from school, and leave it covered for her. And go back to the hospital and start work from six to eight or nine.
(quoted in Webster, 1998, pp.142–3)

For many women like Mrs H who migrated from the Caribbean in the 1950s and 1960s, paid care work in the NHS (as nurses, cooks and cleaners) and day-to-day care responsibilities for children were negotiated in an absence of local frameworks of assistance from friends, family or the community. Class and racial divisions of labour, in which migration played and continues to play a significant part, are therefore central to understanding the different care resources that are available to people in society today.

Attention to the significance of social divisions in the construction of women's lives as well as the ways in which individuals are positioned in local, national and transnational networks of care helps broaden the analytic lens beyond gendered norms about who should 'care'. It brings into focus the experiences of those who provide care in contemporary society. The so-called burdens of care are not experienced equally by women for there are a range of opportunities to minimize or relinquish commitments and responsibilities for those who have the financial resources or support systems. Writing about the USA, Arlie Hochschild (2001) has identified one aspect of this phenomenon as a **global care chain** in which poor migrant women care for the children of richer families while other women, often relatives, provide care for their children in their countries of origin. The social and economic effects of this shift in care for these countries of origin have, however, yet to be fully appreciated.

obal care chain

In Europe, migrant women are increasingly employed in low status, casualized jobs in services such as cleaning, catering and care work (Kofman and Sales, 1998). And, at the same time, the **feminization of migration** and the moral panics about asylum seekers and refugees have forced women into less protected employment, as private nannies and domestic workers, and more dangerous work such as prostitution. This makes them vulnerable to exploitation and gives them few political, economic or social rights (Williams, 2001). Yet such panics about migration do not stem the demand for private domestic services. The numbers of au pairs in the UK are increasing and in 2002 the Labour Government introduced a new initiative to encourage single people under the age of 27, principally from Eastern Europe, into an au pair placement scheme.

feminization of
migration

However, paid domestic work is not just about caring work, it is also concerned with the reproduction of lifestyle, status and identity. As Bridget Anderson (2001, p.6) says, 'Nobody has to have stripped pine floorboards, hand-wash only silk shirts, dust-gathering ornaments'. The employment of migrant women as au pairs and domestic workers – and its support by the state – reinforces class and racialized divides between women but, importantly, also illustrates that the definitions of what constitutes care work and who should provide it are constantly in flux.

3   Theorizing care: questions and dilemmas

To date we have foregrounded how questions about the practices and meanings of care shape our relationships with others, our identities and our sense of self or, in other words, our personal lives. The determination to understand these practices and meanings has resulted in many different approaches to theorizing care. Theories have developed out of the concerns of new social movements and as a result of particular concerns about care because of demographic and economic change. The analysis of care is, therefore, an evolving terrain which, at particular moments, has drawn upon different theoretical perspectives as well as producing new theorizing within and across those perspectives.

The authors in this book also weave a range of perspectives into their analyses. In Chapter 2, Katherine Holden deploys particular elements from feminist and psychoanalytic theory to consider the construction of single women's caring identities. In Chapter 3, Barry Goldson uses social-constructionist, neo-Marxist and feminist approaches to investigate how the law and social policy construct children as 'victims' and 'threats' and the attendant effects of those constructions. And Yasmin Gunaratnam in Chapter 4 explores 'race' and care in the hospice setting, together with questions about the research process, through the lenses of postcolonialism, post-structuralism and feminism. There is not space here to consider in detail each of these perspectives and the valuable insights that they offer the analysis of care relations. We have chosen, therefore, in this introductory chapter, to explore strands concerned with care and welfare in the psychoanalytic tradition, together with feminist perspectives on care that have been developed within social policy and philosophy. As we suggest, these can be understood as having had a particular influence upon policy-making, welfare practice and our personal lives.

3.1   Care and the psychoanalytic tradition

Psychoanalytic approaches have been instrumental in providing concepts and techniques that enable us to recognize and reflect upon the emotional, and especially the unconscious, dimensions of welfare practice (Rustin, 1999). This has been particularly valuable in highlighting what Gunaratnam and Lewis identify as a fundamental contradiction in the provision of social welfare, which they explain in the following way:

> a significant part of the discursive formation of welfare services is that they have been constructed as sites that deal with, and also intervene in matters of the emotional lives of service users – often in highly intimate and 'private' arenas. Yet, bureau-professional imperatives, encompassing both systems (policies, procedures and organizational structures) and practices (action and interactions) are based upon an ambivalent and uneven privileging of rationality over emotion.
>
> (Gunaratnam and Lewis, 2001, p.129)

Because of the centrality of the emotional dimensions of care relations, psychoanalytic theory can be seen as particularly useful in analysing the meanings of care practices. Issues relating to child care, for example, have long been informed by the influences of John Bowlby and Donald Winnicott. During the 1940s and 1950s these two psychoanalysts emphasized that, in terms of human growth and development, the mental health of children was as important to their care and well-being as hygiene and physical health. Bowlby stressed the significance of a 'warm, intimate and continuous relationship with his [the child's] mother (or permanent mother-substitute –

maternal
deprivation
attachment and
loss

one person who steadily 'mothers' him) in which both find satisfaction and enjoyment' (Bowlby, 1953, p.13). A mother's perceived neglect came to be understood as an absence of love and intimacy in her relationship with the child rather than its unwashed clothes, uncombed hair or poor diet. The mother–child bond and the dangers of separation, theorized through notions of **maternal deprivation** and **attachment and loss**, also came to inform professional thinking and practice. This had some beneficial effects on policy-making during the 1950s and 1960s. It brought children's homes and hospitals under scrutiny because, although providing good standards of physical care, they were increasingly understood as not meeting children's emotional and psychological needs. Institutional care for children was reconceptualized to acknowledge that the development of the child's personal identity and relationships depended on sustained emotional attachments. Nowhere is this better illustrated than in the film called *A Two Year Old Goes to Hospital*, directed and filmed by James Robertson, and first shown at the Royal Society of Medicine in 1952.

Figure 1.5   '... quietly clutching her Teddy and "blanket baby", not crying or demanding attention ...' (*A Two Year Old Goes to Hospital* by James Robertson)

As Extract 1.5 illustrates, the influence of the film was significant for it demonstrated unequivocally that children were persons in their own right and vulnerable to the effects of distress and unhappiness.

> ### Extract 1.5   The distress of children in hospital
>
> The point was well made by Ronald MacKeith, a sympathetic paediatrician. 'The film', he remarked, 'opens our eyes to the quiet unhappiness that a young child in hospital may suffer much of the day, almost unnoticed by the nurses and doctors. We do not see the grief and we see only a "good" quiet child. If a child is crying, we may equate this ... to the crying of a small child who is hungry or has fallen. We tend to dismiss all crying as unimportant'. And, he added, 'doctors, nurses and parents all do well to give a child, however small, credit for understanding – or feeling – what is said or felt.
>
> (quoted in Hendrick, 2003, p.230)

This recognition of the child as an individual with strong emotional connections to others, not least to its mother, had several outcomes. It led to the Platt Report (1959), which recommended that mothers be allowed to stay with their children if hospitalized. More generally, there was an appreciation of the child as a 'person' with its own identity, sense of self, and sets of psychic, social and emotional relations as well as rights (Hendrick, 2003). As a result, the personal lives of children increasingly became a focus of policy in the UK. They informed the development of the child welfare movement in the 1950s together with the emerging profession of social work. Interventions in family life – because of children's juvenile delinquency, truancy or mental health – were particularly concerned with the provision of appropriate forms of care which children were understood to need from their parents but, in particular, from their mothers.

In the domestic domain, family life and relationships between mothers and their children were also increasingly shaped by these psychoanalytic approaches to child care. They had become popularized as a result of Winnicott's writings in women's magazines and his regular broadcasts on BBC radio, and the widely available books of US child care expert, Dr Benjamin Spock (1946). However, as Diane Richardson (1993) has pointed out, this shift in understanding child development represented a redefinition of motherhood which foregrounded a woman's 'natural' love for her child together with an instinctive knowledge about how to care for it. Unlike the 1920s and 1930s, mothers were no longer expected to learn the skills of looking after their children from child care experts (see Chapter 2), but simply to draw upon their 'natural' maternal instincts. As section 3.1.1 suggests, this was not unproblematic for many mothers.

There is now little explicit application of psychoanalytic approaches to social work practice since social workers came under increasing criticism from the left during the 1960s and 1970s 'for giving a pathologizing, psychological explanation of deprivations whose origins were held to be material and class based' (Rustin, 1999, p.267). There has remained, however, an interest in using psychoanalytic theory to explore the relation between the rational and emotional in social care organizations and institutions. For example, in the context of care relationships, psychoanalysis brings to the field a recognition that 'normal' life transitions, such as the birth of a child, illness or the death of a friend, can provoke in some individuals unconscious anxieties that have to be recognized and managed by clients, patients and practitioners (**Lucey, 2004**). Such an understanding has the potential to allow both unpaid carers and care professionals opportunities to acknowledge and engage with those anxieties while, at the same time, appreciating the difficulties of managing their own feelings evoked through that process (Rustin, 1999).

The issue of unconscious anxiety has also been analysed through its effects within institutions. The work of Isabel Menzies Lyth (1988, p.63) has shown how nurses and student nurses dealt with experiences of anxiety, guilt and doubt by 'eliminating situations, events, tasks, activities and relationships that cause anxiety or, more correctly, evoke anxieties'. They **defended** themselves against unconscious anxieties provoked through their work. Menzies Lyth points to the way in which a combination of patterns of work, hierarchical structures and a reduction of individual distinctiveness through, for example, wearing a uniform, distances nursing staff from developing close relationships with patients and their relatives. She writes of the working conditions of nurses in the 1970s:

defended

> It is hardly too much to say that the nurse does not nurse patients. The total workload of a ward or department is broken down into lists of tasks, each of which is allocated to a particular nurse. She performs her patient-centred tasks for a large number of patients – perhaps as many as all the patients in the ward, often thirty or more. As a corollary, she performs only a few tasks for, and has restricted contact with, any one patient. This prevents her from coming into contact with the totality of any one patient and his [*sic*] illness and offers some protection from the anxiety this arouses.
>
> (Menzies Lyth, 1988, p.51)

Nursing practices have undergone many changes since this research was undertaken, not least through attempts to provide patients with a 'named nurse' who is expected to provide continuity of care. It is likely, however, that other defences against unconscious anxiety have been constructed alongside changes in work patterns within hospitals. Extract 1.6, from research by Chris Mawson, provides one example of how this might occur in one-to-one relationships between patient and professional.

Extract 1.6   Marie

Marie, a young physiotherapist in the Walsingham Child Health Team, described her visits to the home of a small child with a deformed hand. Each time she went, she knew the treatment would cause the child intense pain. It was clearly saddening for Marie to see the child freeze and turn away from her as soon as she set foot in the family home. She began to adopt a brusque and matter-of-fact manner with both child and mother, at times being quite aware that she was being cold and impermeable, but for the most part conscious only of a heavy sense of persecution and dread whenever she visited. She felt ashamed and defensive whenever she discussed the child and her treatment with other members of the team, and came to feel that this one case was

> casting a shadow over her enjoyment of her work. To protect herself against her guilt, she tried to tell herself that she was only adopting an appropriately professional distance, and that the occasional reproaches from the child's mother were really evidence of the mother's inappropriate need for closeness with Marie.
>
> (Mawson, 1994, p.68)

As the vignette above illustrates, an acknowledgement of the defences constructed against the difficulties of providing care in particular situations allows us to appreciate the effects of these defences upon our everyday encounters with, and relationships to, welfare work, practices and provision (**Newman and Mooney, 2004**). In turn, such an appreciation opens up opportunities to consider the effects of unconscious anxieties upon the personal lives of welfare professionals and clients alike.

ACTIVITY 1.5

Think of a social or health care setting – for example a doctor's surgery, benefits office, educational institution or hospital clinic – in which you have experienced defences against unconscious anxiety. These might have been a professional's, a patient's or a client's.

■ What feelings were invoked in you by this encounter?

■ How did you manage your feelings?

■ Why do you think those defences were being constructed?

COMMENT

The use of psychoanalytic approaches in the analysis of welfare practices offers insights into the patterns of behaviour, feelings, relationships and emotional connections (or absence of them) within institutions. However, as Katherine Holden illustrates in Chapter 2, they can be equally valuable in the interrogation of individual meanings afforded to practices of care that take place within and across the boundaries of familial relationships.

3.1.1 Challenges and critiques

Psychoanalytic approaches to the analysis of care relations have not, however, been without their critics. As we suggested earlier, the redefinition of motherhood, which resulted from the work of Bowlby and Winnicott, was difficult for some women. The emphasis on women's 'natural' abilities to mother and the importance of the mother–child bond meant that some women experienced feelings of inadequacy or guilt if they did not feel a close emotional connection to their child, or if they preferred paid employment to full-time motherhood. Indeed, many feminists in the late 1960s and 1970s perceived Bowlby's work as oppressive to women, claiming that his emphasis on 'natural' abilities of mothering and his idealization of motherhood served to reinforce the gendered roles of women and men in contemporary society. In particular, feminist critiques focused upon the heterosexual nuclear family as the key site where normative assumptions about women's abilities and responsibilities were clustered and where, as a result, their personal lives were shaped and constrained. They argued that welfare policies and practices were built around an expectation that family life could be sustained through the 'natural' disposition of women to care for their children despite the simultaneous demand for women to enter the workforce (**Mooney, 2004b**).

Moreover, the essentializing constructions of gender categories that run through the meanings and practices of child care developed in 1940s and 1950s continue to exert their influences today as we explore in section 4. There remains a general shortage of child care places in the UK despite the huge growth of women in the workplace and a rapid expansion of the child care sector in recent years. There are still only places for 'a minority of children under the age of 8 years (1 in 7 by 2001, compared with 1 in 9 in 1997)' (Land, 2002, p.19). It might be argued that one explanation for this shortage is the tenacious hold that assumptions about the effects of attachment and loss upon young children have had, not only upon child care policy and practice, but also on mothers making decisions about work and child care. For instance, most working mothers in the UK would prefer care of their children to be provided by someone they know or a close family member, while child care provision funded by the state is concentrated upon children who are at least 3 years old. However, the continuing influences of these ideas about child development upon mothers in the negotiation of their personal lives, and policy-makers' perceptions about 'appropriate' child care provision, remain largely unacknowledged in analyses of contemporary child care arrangements and policy formations.

3.2   Feminist approaches to care

During the 1960s and 1970s, feminists were influential in foregrounding the conflicts in women's personal lives as they negotiated the pleasures and frustrations of motherhood. By the 1980s however, the focus upon mothers shifted and feminist theory and research moved into a wider analysis of care relations within families (Finch and Groves, 1983). This was predominantly concerned with care giving and the ways in which women's familial roles, such as wife, mother, sister or daughter, were constructed around gendered assumptions that they would take on unpaid caring responsibilities for family members. As Mary Daly (2002, p.252) has pointed out, this meant that the concept of care was used by feminists to draw attention to 'the material and ideological processes which make up care and at the same time confirm women in the social role of carer. How women's lives revolve around care was explored in a scholarship that was informed by, in the first instance, women's oppression and, in the second, gender'. This scholarship highlighted the important distinction between biological and social reproduction in the nuclear family and emphasized its significance for analyses of care.

Extract 1.7   Biological and social reproduction

Biological and social reproduction become confused: the function of bearing children (biological reproduction) and the emotional bonds that are associated with it become indissolubly linked with the tasks of servicing, maintaining and succouring the domestic group (social reproduction) within which childbearing takes place ... the role of the mother in relation to her children is extended into other relationships and other contexts. In the 'extra-normal' situation of a child being chronically dependent beyond the constraints of dependency dictated by its age – through sickness and impairment – the mother automatically extends and is expected to extend her 'caring for' function. This then becomes the expected norm in relation to their non-child kinfolk in conditions of extra-normal dependency. Just as the affective links that form at birth are tied into the mechanical links of servicing and maintenance in the case of healthy children, the same affective links in the case of disabled and chronically dependent family members similarly get tied to the servicing and maintenance functions.

(Dalley, 1996, p.15)

How do you understand the differences between biological and social reproduction?

This emphasis on the care services provided through the social relations of marriage and kinship has shifted significantly in recent years and a more theoretically sophisticated consideration of the meanings of care has developed. In particular, the concept of care has become central to some feminist analyses of the form and nature of the contemporary welfare state (Daly and Lewis, 2000). There has been particular interest among feminist researchers about the ways in which policy-makers have understood and responded to changes in the demand for and supply of care as a result of demographic, economic and social change over the past twenty years. Such work has illustrated the extent to which the established, but never universal,

male breadwinner model – in which men were constructed as having primary responsibility to provide financially for their families while women were expected to care for them – no longer carries the same prescriptive weight in policy-making in either the UK or Europe. This is thought to be due (in part) to significant changes in behaviour, not least the growing numbers of women entering the labour market and the increasing diversity of family and intimate relationships, which are not based upon the nuclear family model. Jane Lewis (2001) has argued that European governments, but particularly the UK and the Netherlands, are moving towards a new model on which to base policy-making. This is defined as an **adult–worker model** where families are understood to have both partners engaged in full-time work and economically independent of one another. However, in the context of care, this model fails to address the role that many women as adult workers continue to have in providing care to family members, and the poor pay and low status that is given to care work in the employment market (Lewis, 2001).

Such feminist analyses of the intersections of care and paid work within modern welfare regimes have developed a strong comparative element which

male breadwinner model

adult–worker model

builds on other important work in the field of comparative social policy (Cochrane et al., 2001; Ginsburg, 1992). Particular emphasis has been placed on illustrating the enormous variations in the forms and provision of care for children and older people, not only between but also within different European countries (Lewis, 2000). This has demonstrated that people's access to health care, personal care and social care is dependent not just upon country, but also the neighbourhood, town or region in which they live. Such research has usefully highlighted that the UK's struggle to negotiate the relationship between care, employment and social policy is not unique and that no 'modern welfare regime has found a way of valuing the caring work performed by women in the family' (Lewis, 2000, p.41). But much of this comparative work tends to use abstract models (Sainsbury, 1994, 1999) and statistical data to construct its arguments. As a result, there is little published empirical research that compares the different ways in which variations between welfare systems might constitute personal lives.

Work by researchers such as Prue Chamberlayne (1999), who engages implicitly with feminist theory and explicitly with biographical methods, has begun to open up the field of comparative social policy. Chamberlayne's analysis of care relations in Bremen, Leipzig and London, considers how the relationship between the 'private' and 'public' spheres was structured differently in the three societies and the effects of these structures upon carers' everyday practices. She summarizes the findings in the following way:

Extract 1.8   Cultures of care

In the *Cultures of Care* study we found a powerful sense of home ties and of family responsibilities and identities in all three societies. Both women carers and male spouse carers were determined to sustain central caring roles, including in circumstances of great personal sacrifice. In all three societies there were some carers who were mainly confined to the home sphere, some who were more outwardly oriented, and some who were torn between home and the outside world. However, the interplay of personal factors/family pressures and service contexts which produced a particular orientation was markedly different in each society, as were the individual motivations for each strategy ... [T]he variations between cases in each country were often as helpful as the contrasts between societies, since the carers who resisted or worked around particular constraints and pressures often highlighted those very structures.

(Chamberlayne, 1999, p.156)

---

empirical research   Extract 1.8 demonstrates the extent to which **empirical research** can bring the interconnections of personal lives and social policy into sharp focus. Biographical interviews, such as those conducted by Chamberlayne with carers, allow individuals to construct narratives through which they can make sense of their welfare encounters. Such narratives can illustrate opportunities to accept or resist particular welfare interventions and the effects of these opportunities upon an individual's sense of agency. Take, for instance, Mrs Rushton, who was interviewed as part of Chamberlayne's study, and her complaint that 'Your life is run without you having any say in it. You are beholden to them ... I sometimes feel I am taken over ... they're coming in on my personal privacy' (Chamberlayne, 1999, p.164). Narratives might also demonstrate a refusal by the interviewee to be constituted as a particular welfare subject, such as a 'carer' or 'disabled person'. Regardless of the experience being narrated, this type of research evidence offers valuable insights into how personal lives are constructed and negotiated through welfare discourses and practices.

ACTIVITY 1.6

Take some time here to reflect on the practical and methodological difficulties that might be encountered in doing comparative research where biographical interviews with carers are conducted in different European countries. How might those difficulties impact upon the collection of research evidence, its analysis and the possibility of drawing generalized conclusions?

COMMENT

Biographical interviews clearly offer opportunities to explore the differential experiences of welfare at local and regional levels, which then allow for comparisons across and below the level of the nation-state. However, there are difficulties where comparative research is being conducted with small numbers of research subjects, which is often the case with in-depth interviews. It is possible that the degrees of difference between individual experiences, or the different use of particular terms to explain those experiences, are so great that comparison proves impossible. It may be that a determination to find similarities of experience means that wider political, social or cultural differences of context are lost.

In what ways might our earlier point about the historical and cultural specificity of the concept of carer be relevant here?

Despite these potential limitations, the use of interviews as research evidence ensures that the individual is located at the centre of both the research process and its analysis. In turn, the experiences and concerns of their personal lives are also brought into sharp relief. This is illustrated in more detail in the following chapters where each author uses interview extracts from their own research projects to explore the dynamic of 'the personal' and wider sets of welfare relations and structures.

It is not only in comparative social policy that feminist theorizing has revealed new ways of thinking and exploring 'the personal' in the context of care. There has also been a significant development which has focused upon the elaboration of the non-material basis of care (Daly, 2002). This means that the focus of research for some feminists has shifted from the analysis of care relations in particular locations or between individuals to a more philosophical consideration of care as a moral and political concept that can inform ethical practice and behaviour in society. So, for example, Yasmin Gunaratnam uses the importance of ethical practice and behaviour to develop the idea of care as **ethic of care**   an analytic practice in Chapter 4. The notion of an **ethic of care** has also developed. It is perceived by feminists as a set of values that can guide human agency in a variety of social fields (Sevenhuijsen, 2000). As an ontological project, the emphasis has been upon care as a way of being in the world. There has been a shift from conceptualizing care as being simply based in networks of family and kin relationships to an acknowledgement that care relations connect people throughout society. In such theorizing, *caring about* is as significant to conceptualizing care as *taking care of* and *being cared for* (Daly, 2002), and it foregrounds the mutual interdependence of our care relationships since, at some level, we are all givers and receivers of care. Interdependence is consequently seen as the basis of human interactions as Fiona Williams explains:

> in these terms, autonomy and independence are about the capacity for self-determination rather than the expectation of individual self-sufficiency. It recognizes that vulnerability is a human condition and that some people are constituted as more or less vulnerable than others, at different times and in different places.
>
> (Williams, 2001, p.487)

Feminists' understanding of an ethic of care is, therefore, frequently set in opposition to an *ethic of justice*, which is understood as being underpinned by a notion of individual rights and an *ethic of work*, which plays such a central role in constructing our values, rights and duties today (Williams, 2000; **Mooney, 2004b**).

It is for these reasons that Williams (2001) has argued for the inclusion of an ethics of care alongside an ethics of work as the basis of citizenship. This would mean that care of the self and care of others are no longer understood as having to fit around the demands of work space and time, but are recognized as important and valuable activities in their own right. The values of care – responsibility, trust, tolerance for human limitations and frailties and acceptance of diversity – would also be used to extend the conceptualization of citizenship and its boundaries.

3.2.1 Challenges and critiques

The themes and emphases of feminist research have not, however, been universally accepted. Moreover, silences and absences have also been identified by both feminist writers and others working in the discipline of social policy. Writing in 1991, Hilary Graham critiqued the ways in which care as a concept had been used and developed by British feminists in their early work. She noted the focus on one form of care (unpaid by relatives) and one structural division (gender), which left divisions based on class and 'race' out of the analytic lens and elided the work of carers in the homes of people to whom they are not related. More recent feminist research has expanded analyses of the terrain of care but, as our discussion in the next section suggests, the assumptions about care and caring identified by Graham continue to dominate both policy practice and provision. Normative assumptions about women providing care and 'the family' as the site of care remain deeply embedded in analyses of care within social policy as indicated in the following quotation from *Key Concepts and Debates in Health and Social Policy:* 'In this chapter we turn to the private and public roles of the family, exploring concepts of care and caring. We shall focus on gender as the key to developing understandings of the complex relations between work, family and social care' (Malin et al., 2002, p.111).

As Graham argued, this mode of analysis obscures forms of home-based care that are not based on marriage and kinship obligations and leaves them under-conceptualized as a result. However, more recent research into the practices of care in same-sex intimate relationships has brought fresh insights to the meanings and significance given to care responsibilities in the home. It has shown that 'home' can be understood as more than a private place and that 'it is often about broader communities and a wider set of belongings' (Weeks et al., 2001, p.101).

ACTIVITY 1.7

The quotation below is from an interview and is a comment on the response of one man to the 'crisis' of AIDS:

> [H]e has taken younger boys under his wing ... and he's had three AIDS sufferers whom he's taken into his home and looked after, and he's got one at the moment. I mean, he's not there all the time but you know, he more or less says, 'feel free to stay here whenever you want, whenever you need to. Whenever you need peace and quiet or whatever'.
>
> (M36 quoted in Weeks et al., 2001, p.102)

- How does it illustrate the blurring of boundaries between home and the community?
- In what ways does it disrupt notions of home-based care?
- How might the idea of an ethic of care be used to explain this particular form of care provision?

The norms and omissions in feminist analyses of care have also been highlighted by feminists writing from a disability rights perspective. We have already pointed to some of these in section 2. Jenny Morris (1991), for example, has criticized feminist research and its emphases in a number of key areas. These include: the ways in which the divisions between carer and the receiver of care have been constructed to position the latter as a 'dependent'; the silencing of the voices of the 'cared for' in feminist research; and the obscuring of the rights of disabled people to adequate support which would enable them to make choices in their personal lives.

Further critiques were developed over the issue of young carers, which had become the focus of increasing policy and public interest in the mid 1990s. In Extract 1.9, Lois Keith and Jenny Morris highlight that problematizing families with a disabled parent fails to acknowledge the interdependent nature of *all* family life and suggests that disability precludes good parenting.

> ### Extract 1.9   Care, disability and parenting
>
> ... much of the thinking around the issue of children who are 'carers' has trouble distinguishing between parenting – the concern and sense of responsibility that parents have for their children's welfare in all its manifestations – and the practical and physical things which adults do when looking after children and running a home ... those involved in researching these issues perhaps need reminding that a disabled parent's ability to love and care for their children is not dependent on them being able to perform all the physical tasks that other parents might do.
>
> (Keith and Morris, 1995, p.41)

The various challenges to feminist theorizing of care reflect the contested and complex nature of care relations. As a whole, however, this section has suggested that a continued interrogation of the meanings, values and assumptions embedded in theories and analyses of care is required if we are to ensure that the needs for care, desires to care and responsibilities of care in our personal lives are acknowledged and addressed in social policy.

4   Welfare, care and personal lives

As our discussion has illustrated so far, many of the meanings of care have been implicitly and explicitly connected to norms of marriage and kin relations. Such norms can also be traced through the history of policy-making which, from its origins in the Poor Law Act of 1601, has understood 'the family' to have a moral responsibility and obligation to provide care for its members. Although historical research (Laslett, 1983) has suggested that we cannot assume that there was a Golden Age when families *did* provide the care required for their older, sick and disabled relatives, families have remained central to policy assumptions about caring responsibilities. There

care deficit   have, therefore, been long periods with a clear **care deficit** (Hochschild, 1995), meaning that the need and demand for care could not be reconciled with available sources of care.

As the range and extent of social policy expanded through the twentieth century, perceptions about which groups in society deserved care, through either financial or practical support, broadened as did the moral justifications for their inclusion into the welfare community (Morris, 1998). Nevertheless, political and social fears about the ability and willingness of families to meet the responsibilities to care for their dependants has continued to shape policy-making, as have concerns about the demands of care provision upon public spending. The state may acknowledge some responsibility for ensuring the physical and mental well-being of its citizens but, at the same time, it has always sought to define clearly the boundaries of that responsibility.

The Beveridge Report (1942) provides an excellent example of how these boundaries are always in the process of construction and reconstruction. In keeping with the priorities of the newly elected Labour Government of 1945,

Beveridge, a Liberal, acknowledged that 'the community' had to take on greater responsibilities in constructing the new post-war society, but he also held fast to older ideas about individual responsibility as shown in Extract 1.10.

> **Extract 1.10   Beveridge: defining individual responsibilities**
>
> It is a logical corollary to the receipt of high benefits in disability that the individual should recognize the duty to be well and to co-operate in all steps which may lead to diagnosis of disease in early stages when it can be prevented. Disease and accident must be paid for in any case, in lessened power of production and in idleness, if not directly by insurance benefits. One of the reasons why it is preferable to pay for disease and accident openly and directly in the form of insurance benefits, rather than indirectly, is that it emphasizes the cost and should give a stimulus to prevention.
>
> (Beveridge, 1942, p.158)

These deliberations on the development of health and rehabilitation services are both imbued with this idea of personal responsibility and tied to notions of
worker–citizen
the **worker–citizen** and his [*sic*] rights and needs (**Lewis and Fink, 2004**). We can see that Beveridge's proposal to extend the forms of statutory entitlement and provision available to disabled and ill people was shaped by a moral judgement about their possible rights and needs. This judgement focused upon the financial costs of meeting those needs rather than the effects of illness and disability upon the individual's personal well-being and sense of
deserving
self. The **deserving** nature of their claims was thus seemingly held in doubt because of uncertainty about their employability so, although not categorized
undeserving
as **undeserving**, their position in the UK's new post-war welfare society
post-war
remained somewhat ambiguous. However, one of the results of the **post-war**
settlement
settlement (Hughes and Lewis, 1998) was a redrawing of these moral boundaries in which the deservingness of older, sick and disabled people began to be defined in medical terms, with the result that they were no longer perceived as being morally responsible for their incapacity.

4.1   Care and the community

With a strong economy, the post-war welfare state saw a rapid expansion in the provision of health and social services in the community as expectations grew, the numbers of older people in the population rose (**Widdowson, 2004**) and long-stay institutions were slowly closed. But by the 1980s, the influences of Thatcherism and concerns at the 'drain' on public expenditure, particularly in the support of older people in residential and nursing homes, caused a major reassessment of the social services budget. The first move was the Conservative Government's policy towards statutory care provision, which emphasized the importance of care by the community rather than care in the community. However, as feminists quickly pointed out, this essentially meant care by the family and, in particular, care by women. A series of reports followed, including the Audit Commission's *Making a Reality of Community*

Care in 1986, which criticized the fragmented nature of care services, and the Griffiths Report in 1988. In the latter, there were two controversial but ultimately highly influential proposals. These were 'that social services should become "enabling agencies", restricting their role as far as possible to procuring and overseeing care and not its provision, and that central government should be closely involved in determining the priorities of a costed programme each year of its funding' (Hadley and Clough, 1997, p.15). Significantly, for meanings of care and its provision, these proposals were accepted and incorporated into the National Health Service and Community Care Act in 1990.

'S NO GOOD TRYING TO
ILD A RELATIONSHIP
TH ME – I'M DUE TO
REPLACED BY A
RE COST-EFFECTIVE
ODEL

re 1.6

There is an enormous literature on the subject of this Act and its effects upon care provision (Hadley and Clough, 1997; Lewis and Glennerster, 1996), but, because of constraints of space, we are going to focus upon one particular aspect. Community care under the 1990 Act and subsequent legislation has been driven by a managerialist discourse (Clarke and Newman, 1997; Newman, 1998) in which the issues of efficiency and effectiveness constrain and shape the provision and delivery of care to individuals in their homes. This can impact adversely upon the personal lives of clients and workers alike as they struggle to reconcile the realities of care work, with all its messy, time-consuming and emotional components, and the 'disembodied, aetherializing quality' (Twigg, 2000, p.5) of much care policy at both local and national levels. For paid care workers, the negotiation of the boundaries between 'doing care' and 'being caring' is made more complicated by increasingly regimented and regulated work practices and professional regulations (**Newman and Mooney, 2004**). Such regimes fail to acknowledge that the management of 'doing care' cannot be reconciled with the determination of some care workers to be caring.

emotional labour

The emphasis on the efficient delivery of physical activities of care means that the **emotional labour** demands of care work (James, 1992) are rarely equated into the 'care package'. Time spent listening to clients, calming their fears, or negotiating their anger, is assumed to be part of what care workers *do* but not what they are paid for. Equally, the management of the care workers' emotions following distressing or frustrating encounters with clients is seldom considered. This reinforces our earlier point that the boundaries between doing care and being caring are unstable and overlapping.

The permeability of boundaries between labour, love and intimacy are well illustrated in a study of the growth of paid care in the USA where, like the UK, it is 'measured, allocated and monitored by accounting systems, which fragment into countable components' (Stone, 2000, p. 89).

ACTIVITY 1.8

Read Extract 1.11 from Deborah Stone's analysis of her interviews with care workers and consider why these workers resist their employers' regulations.

Extract 1.11   The unstable boundaries of paid care work

Several [workers] tell me that though they are not supposed to give out their home numbers, they do it selectively, or they tell a client, 'I can't give you my number, but if you want to call me it's in the book'. They are also quick to tell me that they do not mind that clients call them and they do not think clients ever abuse the access. When I ask what kinds of things clients call about, the aides make clear that they think every call is legitimate ... [Care workers] feel that giving their clients their phone numbers contributes to good care, but it also clearly violates the rules of the employer. They understand why the agency has this rule. They usually say that the rule is to protect them from excessive demands by clients and to keep their care-giving job within the bounds of a job. But they are not sure they *want* to keep their relationship within the bounds of the job as defined by the agency, or that the agency's boundaries permit them to do the job right ... The problem here is that when caring goes public, when it is done as work instead of as private family or friendship relationships, it suddenly gets new and smaller boundaries. Now, everything in the relationship must be defined as part of the work. If client and care giver spend time together, it is work time and must be compensated and regulated like the rest of work time. But people's relationships jump the boundaries. Their feelings for one another do not stay precisely modulated according to the norms of a professional or employment relationship.

(Stone, 2000, pp.105–6)

Research such as Stone's illustrates how paid care work is shot through with emotions that cannot be regulated by prescriptive employment practices or defined by abstract principles. Care workers' sense of self and their identity as 'caring' refuses the divisions between public and private, between home and work and between paid and unpaid that employers seek to impose. While the regulation of care practices might ultimately encourage dehumanizing practice, because 'making people subject to regimes of efficiency, of standardized responses, inevitably denies their individuality and humanity' (Twigg, 2000, p.120), care workers negotiate and resist such regulations by recognizing the porous boundaries between their personal lives and those of their clients.

4.2   The boundaries of care provision in welfare discourse and practices

The refusal by paid care workers of the boundaries imposed by employers and work practices is significant for understanding another strand in the meanings attributed to care. This is the distinction made by policy-makers between formal and informal care and the nature of its delivery. Such a distinction has three main assumptions inherent to it. First, that informal care is provided, often unpaid, in the home by family members, friends or neighbours. Second, that although informal care in minoritized ethnic communities is largely invisible in policy analyses, it is assumed that African-Caribbean and Asian families 'always look after their own' (Atkin and Rollings, 1996, p.76). And finally, that formal care is supplied by professional health, welfare and child care workers within institutional settings (**Newman and Mooney, 2004**). However, these assumptions have little basis in the context of actual care relations. Many older, sick and disabled people are supported at home through the care of paid workers who may, or may not, consider themselves to be care professionals. The opportunities for Asian people to provide care are shaped by factors such as the availability of appropriate housing, restrictive immigration policies that divide families across continents and the growth in women's paid employment. Among African-Caribbean populations, the numbers of women in paid work is also a significant consideration in their ability to provide care. Moreover, research has demonstrated that informal care is rarely given 'free' – even where provided within the family – and is frequently based on principles of reciprocity and redistribution. This is particularly the case for child-minding arrangements which are negotiated through mutual systems of support between friends, family and neighbours (Land, 2002).

Assumptions by policy-makers about the distinction between the formal and informal sectors of care in the UK, and what is provided by each sector, has resulted in fragmented and, at times, incoherent provision of care for children and older or disabled people. As Hilary Land has pointed out:

> the government rejected the 1999 Royal Commission's majority proposal that personal care should be provided free on the same basis as health care for elderly people. Day care [for children] is to be paid for, subject to a means test in the National Child Care Strategy, while formal education remains a free service for children.
>
> (Land, 2002, p.14)

The distinction being drawn between health and personal (or social) care is an important one in the context of care for older people because it marks the boundary in England and Wales of the state's responsibility for its citizens. Health care, provided for example by GPs and hospitals, remains free at the point of need as established under the National Health Service Act of 1945. But, the provision of social care, which might include help with bathing, dressing or preparing food, is subject to means testing despite intense lobbying by pressure groups and the recommendations of the Royal

Commission on Long Term Care in 1999. In Scotland, the division between health and social care is less clearly drawn, but, with growing economic constraints and a greater demand for personal care than anticipated, stiffer eligibility tests can be expected.

Figure 1.7   Social care provisions

A different divide exists in the field of day care for children, as the quotation above illustrates, in that formal education for children is a free service but other forms of day care are the subject of payment or means testing. Both divides, however, demonstrate the ways that attempts to limit claims on the state are always under construction while other claims, like those to health and education, appear to remain inviolable.

Can you think of reasons why health and education have remained largely 'free' care services?

It is the formal care sector that has predominantly benefited from the policy distinctions between formal and informal care. Subsidies for child care that form part of the Working Families Tax Credit have tended to go to private nurseries, while older and disabled people who receive cash to buy in care services are not allowed to employ relatives to provide those services. Such restrictions have meant that opportunities for informal carers to make decisions about care arrangements have been limited. One of the reasons for the reluctance to acknowledge the day-to-day practices of care in the home and between friends, family and neighbours and the refusal to reward them financially may be an assumption 'that direct financial reward will have a negative effect on the supply as well as the quality of informal care' (Land, 2002, p.15).

We can again trace within this assumption the extent to which informal care is conceptualized as 'natural', with financial reward neither expected nor appropriate. Feminists would argue that such ideological assumptions are embedded within social policy and inform welfare discourses about care relations in the domestic domain, particularly the view that informal care is morally distinct from the pressures of the market that increasingly characterize the formal sector. However, it might be argued that the reluctance to reward those delivering care informally stems from the state's determination to resist further public expenditure. It is likely that an explanation combines elements of ideology and economics, but this idealization of informal care by policy-makers clearly has implications for the personal lives of women since they tend to have the greater number of unpaid care responsibilities for family members.

5   Conclusion

To draw together the themes of this chapter, we have included an extract from an unpublished diary kept by Peter Townsend, the well-known sociologist and researcher into poverty, while he was working as a care assistant in a long-stay institution. This diary formed part of an extensive research project into the care of older people in Britain in the 1960s, which ultimately played a significant part in policy decisions to replace long-stay hospital care.

ACTIVITY 1.9

As you read through Extract 1.12, think about the different issues that have been raised through the chapter. In particular:

■   reflect upon the different meanings of care within the extract;

■   consider the ways in which feminist and psychoanalytic theoretical perspectives might be used to analyse the encounter between the researcher, the care worker and the patient;

■   ask yourself why diaries might provide useful research evidence.

Extract 1.12   Townsend: diary of a care worker

Monday 19th October 1959

12 noon. Reached Newholme, Manchester, a residential home for 515 people, the great majority of them over 65 ... My first job was to help bath [a man] of 72. One of his hands, at the end of a shortened and thin arm, was clenched up tight like a vice. One leg was very emaciated and too short. He had a surgical boot. He had to be lifted into the bath. His voice was slurred. 'I look forward to my bath.' Mr Barton rubbed a flannel (used for everyone) with a small cube of yellow carbolic soap and lathered him gently all over, except for his genitals and backside (curiously, I never saw him wash a man's bottom). He then washed the hair on his balding head with the flannel, placed a couple of towels, which had been used previously, on the floor and another on the chair, and we lifted the man out and sat him in the chair. We took a baggy vest and pair of woollen underpants from the pile on the radiator and then an outsize green shirt – 'I can usually tell the size' – and began to dress [the man]. The shirt had one button missing and the sleeves had to be rolled up. It seemed to have been pressed very badly and was of poor quality. All the collars of the shirts refused to lay down and tended to stick up. A man may get any shirt,

underclothes, socks and trousers, but sometimes his suit was marked with his name. We selected a tie and tied it round his neck. We helped him into a ghastly herringbone tweed suit, the casualty of much cleaning ... I cleaned the man's boots – cracked and white in places with perspiration. Mr Barton handed the man his socks and boots – 'Johnny likes to do what he can for himself. He would do everything if he could' ... We trimmed his toe and finger nails. His grimy tweed cap was the last article to be donned. This was routine. The whole operation took us some 30 or 40 minutes.

... If ever I wanted it, here was compelling evidence against the large institution. Every man who was bathed knew what was expected of him. He had to be as quick as humanly possible, he had to submit to whatever was done or proposed. He never commented on the water, whether it was too cold (as I would certainly have said) on the soap, on the flannel, or on the towels (which were much too small) ... A man was washed in public. There was no physical secret which could be kept secret.

(Townsend, 1959, pp.1–5)

This passage about the bathing of a disabled man touches on many of the issues and themes that we have explored in this chapter. It illustrates the ways in which care practices unsettle so many of the boundaries through which we understand and organize our social relations. We can see that Newholme, as a site of care, was Mr Barton's place of *work*, but it was *home* to the man being bathed. Unlike our more usual experiences of washing and bathing, in Newholme it was a *public* task and not shaped by *private* preferences or pleasures. Moreover, as the passage suggests, *places* of care – such as residential homes – cannot always be equally defined as caring *spaces* despite the best intentions of the staff.

Extract 1.12 also points to the dimensions of *power* and *control* that can be embedded in care relations. The man being bathed and dressed was not able to make decisions about how, when and where he was washed and, equally, he could not make choices about his clothes. He was allowed minimal opportunities for *independence* and was infantilized both through Mr Barton's physical control of the situation and by being addressed in the third person (by his first name).

The themes raised in our discussion of theoretical approaches to analysing care can be traced, too, in this account. We can see how the psychoanalytic notion of *unconscious anxiety* could be used to analyse the actions of Mr Barton, as carer, and the responses of Peter Townsend, as researcher. Such analysis would suggest that Mr Barton constructed *defences* against his own anxieties about disability, ageing and dependency by maintaining procedures and routines that allowed him to avoid not only emotional involvement but also intimate physical contact with the man being bathed. It would propose that Peter Townsend's anxieties were expressed through his angry and emphatic detailing of the inadequacy of the material resources in Newholme and the inability of people living there to make choices or decisions about even the most mundane of activities. From the feminist theorizing considered earlier, we could analyse the care relations in Newholme using, for example, an *ethic of care*. Such an analysis would argue that the care practices in this institution demonstrate how crucial it is that the autonomy, dignity and independence of the person receiving care is recognized and that the principles of choice, quality, user control and variety underpin care provision (Williams, 2001).

Such analyses are considerably aided by the careful attention to detail in the extract and the resultant wealth of evidence it provides about care provisions at Newholme. However, the diary formed just one element in Peter Townsend's *ethnographic* study of the nature of care for older people in institutions and homes during the 1950s. He also conducted interviews with staff and residents, worked as a care assistant, drew plans of homes and took photographs of bedrooms, dining rooms and lounges in the care homes to illustrate the living conditions of residents. The result was a very powerful collection of *research evidence* that became instrumental in changing the nature and form of statutory provision for older people requiring care. *Empirical research* has thus been particularly valuable in tracing the fine detail of the effects of policy-making upon the personal lives of people giving and receiving care.

In conclusion, then, this brief account of the bathing of a disabled man demonstrates the complex and multi-layered meanings of care that we have emphasized throughout the chapter. It helps us see that the personal lives of Mr Barton, Peter Townsend and 'Johnny' became intertwined through this activity which positioned one man as vulnerable and needy and the others as powerful and controlling. It highlights that the practices and relations of care construct a web of emotional, physical and psychological connections between welfare users, welfare workers and researchers that influentially shape their sense of self and their (perhaps overlapping) identities as 'user', 'worker' and 'researcher'. As the chapters that follow also demonstrate, these are complicated connections but they are central to understanding how care is a central feature in the mutual constitution of personal lives and social policy.

Further resources

The issue of care has been the focus of much academic interest and there is an extensive literature as a result. David Morgan provides a useful overview of the developments in thinking about the relationship between family, gender and care in *Family Connections* (1996) and Lynn Jamieson's *Intimacy* (1998) illustrates how care and love intersect in different ways in relationships between parents and children, families, sexual partners, couples and friends. For a detailed consideration of the changing nature of children's care, you could look at *Rethinking Children's Care* (2003) which is edited by Jill Brannen and Peter Moss. If you want to explore further issues relating to professional care practice, Jill Reynolds et al. (2003) have put together a valuable collection of different perspectives on care management and the management of care in *The Managing Care Reader*. In the context of relationships between users of services, professionals and managers, you may also find Lynn Froggett's psychosocial approach in *Love, Hate and Welfare* (2002) very interesting.

The following websites may also be useful (all were accessed on 7 September 2003):

http://www.carers.gov.uk
This provides some context for the present Labour Government's support of carers through its 'Caring for Carers' initiative.

http://www.carers.org
This is the website of the Princess Royal Trust for Carers and it illustrates how one of the many voluntary caring organizations offers support and advice to carers.

http://www.leeds.ac.uk/cava/
'Care, Values and the Future of Welfare' is a major research project that is made up of a number of different studies into the changing nature of care in contemporary society. The website provides insights into the concerns and interests of research in this area.

References

Ackers, L. and Dwyer, P. (2002) *Senior Citizenship? Retirement, Migration and Welfare in the European Union*, Bristol, The Policy Press.

Anderson, B. (2001) 'Reproductive labour and migration', Paper presented at the Sixth Metropolis Conference, Rotterdam.

Arber, S. and Ginn, J. (1990) 'The meaning of informal care: gender and the contribution of elderly people', *Ageing and Society*, vol.10, no.4, pp.429–54.

Atkin, K. and Rollings, J. (1996) 'Looking after their own? Family care-giving among Asian and Afro-Caribbean communities' in Ahmad, W.I.U. and Atkin, K. (eds) *Race and Community Care*, Buckingham, Open University Press.

Audit Commission (1986) *Making a Reality of Community Care*, London, HMSO.

Barnes, M. (1997) *Care, Communities and Citizens*, London, Longman.

Becker, S., Dearden, C. and Aldridge, J. (2001) 'Children's labour of love? Young carers and care work' in Mizen, P., Pole, C. and Bolton, A. (eds) *Hidden Hands: International Perspectives on Children's Work and Labour*, London, Routledge.

Beveridge, W. (1942) *Social Insurance and Allied Services* (The Beveridge Report), Cmnd 6404, London, HMSO.

Bowlby, J. (1953) *Child Care and the Growth of Love*, Harmondsworth, Penguin.

Brannen, J. and Moss, P. (2003) *Rethinking Children's Care*, Buckingham, Open University Press.

Bytheway, B. and Johnson, J. (1998) 'The social construction of "carers"' in Symonds, A. and Kelly, A. (eds) *The Social Construction of Community Care*, London, Macmillan.

Carabine, J. (ed.) (2004) *Sexualities: Personal Lives and Social Policy*, Bristol, The Policy Press in association with The Open University.

Chamberlayne, P. (1999) 'Cultural analysis of the informal sphere' in Chamberlayne et al. (eds) (1999).

Chamberlayne, P., Cooper, A., Freeman, R. and Rustin, M. (eds) (1999) *Welfare and Culture in Europe: Towards a New Paradigm in Social Policy*, London, Jessica Kingsley.

Clarke, J. and Newman, J. (1997) *The Managerial State*, London, Sage.

Cochrane, A., Clarke, J. and Gewirtz, S. (eds) (2001) *Comparing Welfare States*, London, Sage.

Dalley, G. (1996) *Ideologies of Caring: Rethinking Community and Collectivism*, London, Macmillan.

Daly, M. (2002) 'Care as a good for social policy', *Journal of Social Policy*, vol.31, no.2, pp.251–70.

Daly, M. and Lewis, J. (2000) 'The concept of social care and the analysis of contemporary welfare states', *British Journal of Sociology*, vol.51, no.2, pp.281–98.

Finch, J. and Groves, H. (eds) (1983) *A Labour of Love: Women, Work and Caring*, London, Routledge and Kegan Paul.

Froggett, L. (2002) *Love, Hate and Welfare: Psychosocial Approaches to Policy and Practice*, Bristol, The Policy Press.

Ginsburg, N. (1992) *Divisions of Welfare: A Critical Introduction of Comparative Social Policy*, London, Sage.

Graham, H. (1983) 'Caring: a labour of love' in Finch and Groves (eds) (1983).

Graham, H. (1991) 'The concept of caring in feminist research: the case of domestic service', *Sociology*, vol.25, no.1, pp.61–78.

Gunaratnam, Y. (1991) *Call For Care*, London, Health Education Authority, Kings Fund Centre.

Gunaratnam, Y. (1993) 'Beyond caring: towards a feminist re-conceptualization of care', unpublished MSc dissertation, University of London.

Gunaratnam, Y. and Lewis, G. (2001) 'Racializing emotional labour and emotionalizing racialized labour: anger, fear and shame in social welfare', *Journal of Social Work Practice*, vol.15, no.2, pp.125–42.

Hadley, R. and Clough, R. (1997) *Care in Chaos: Frustration and Challenge in Community Care*, London, Cassell.

Harris, J. (2002) 'Caring for citizenship', *British Journal of Social Work*, vol.32, no.3, pp.267–81.

Hendrick, H. (2003) 'Children's emotional well-being and mental health in early post-Second World War Britain: the case of unrestricted hospital visiting' in Gijswijt-Hofstra, M. and Marland, H. (eds) *Cultures of Child Health in Britain and the Netherlands in the Twentieth Century*, Amsterdam, Rodopi.

Hochschild, A. (1995) 'The culture of politics: traditional, postmodern, cold-modern, and warm-modern ideals of care', *Social Politics. International Studies in Gender, State and Society,* vol.2, no.3, pp.331–46.

Hochschild, H. (2001) 'Global care chains and emotional surplus value' in Hutton, W. and Giddens, A. (eds) *On the Edge: Living with Global Capitalism*, London, Vintage.

Hoggett, P. (2000) 'Social policy and the emotions' in Lewis et al. (eds) (2000).

Hughes, G. and Lewis, G. (eds) (1998) *Unsettling Welfare: The Reconstruction of Social Policy*, London, Routledge.

James, N. (1992) 'Care=Organization + physical labour + emotional labour', *Sociology of Health and Illness*, vol.14, no.4, pp.448–509.

Jamieson, L. (1998) *Intimacy: Personal Relationships in Modern Societies*, Cambridge, Polity Press.

Keith, L. and Morris, J. (1995) 'Easy targets: a disability rights perspective on the "children as carers" debate', *Critical Social Policy*, vol.15, no.45, pp.36–57.

Kestenbaum, A. (1999) *What Price Independence? Independent Living and People with High Support Needs*, Bristol, The Policy Press.

Kofman, E. and Sales, R. (1998) 'Migrant women and exclusion in Europe', *The European Journal of Women's Studies*, vol.5, issue 3/4, pp.381–98.

Land, H. (2002) 'Spheres of care in the UK: separate and unequal', *Critical Social Policy*, vol.22, no.1, pp.13–32.

Laslett, P. (1983) *The World We Have Lost – Further Explored* (3rd edn), London, Methuen.

Lewis, G. (ed.) (2004) *Citizenship: Personal Lives and Social Policy*, Bristol, The Policy Press in association with The Open University.

Lewis, G. and Fink, J. (2004) 'All that heaven allows: the worker citizen in the post-war welfare state' in Lewis (ed.) (2004).

Lewis, G., Gewirtz, S. and Clarke, J. (eds) (2000) *Rethinking Social Policy*, London, Sage.

Lewis, J. (2000) 'Gender and welfare regimes' in Lewis et al. (eds) (2000).

Lewis, J. (2001) 'The decline of the male breadwinner model: implications for work and care', *Social Politics*, vol.8, no.2, pp.152–69.

Lewis, J. and Glennerster, H. (1996) *Implementing the New Community Care*, Buckingham, Open University Press.

Lloyd, L. (2000) 'Caring about carers: only half the picture?', *Critical Social Policy*, vol.20, no.1, pp.136–50.

Lucey, H. (2004) 'Differentiated citizenship: psychic defence, social division and the construction of local secondary school markets' in Lewis (ed.) (2004).

Malin, N., Wilmot, S. and Manthorpe, J. (2002) *Key Concepts in Health and Social Policy*, Buckingham, Open University Press.

Mawson, C. (1994) 'Contained anxiety in work with damaged children' in Obholzer, A. and Roberts, V. (eds) *The Unconscious at Work: Individual and Organizational Stress in the Human Services*, London, Routledge.

Menzies Lyth, I. (1988) *Containing Anxiety in Institutions*, London, Free Association Books.

Ministry of Health (1959) *The Welfare of Children in Hospital* (The Platt Report), London, HMSO.

Mooney, G. (ed.) (2004a) *Work: Personal Lives and Social Policy*, Bristol, The Policy Press in association with The Open University.

Mooney, G. (2004b) 'Towards a social policy of work' in Mooney (ed.) (2004).

Morgan, D.H.J. (1996) *Family Connections*, Cambridge, Polity Press.

Morris, J. (1991) *Pride Against Prejudice*, London, Women's Press.

Morris, L. (1998) 'Legitimate membership of the welfare community' in Langan, M. (ed.) *Welfare: Needs, Rights and Risks*, London, Routledge.

Newman, J. (1998) 'Managerialism and social welfare' in Hughes, G. and Lewis, G. (eds) (1998).

Newman, J. and Mooney, G. (2004) 'Managing personal lives: doing "welfare work"' in Mooney (ed.) (2004).

Reynolds, J., Henderson, J., Seden, J., Charlesworth, J. and Bullman, A. (eds) (2003) *The Managing Care Reader*, London, Routledge.

Richardson, D. (1993) *Women, Motherhood and Childrearing*, London, Macmillan.

Robertson, J. (1953) *A Two Year Old Goes to Hospital*, http://www. robertsonfilms.info (accessed 4 December 2003). (Available from Concorde Video and Film Council.)

Rustin, M. (1999) 'Missing dimensions in the culture of welfare' in Chamberlayne et al. (eds) (1999).

Sainsbury, D. (ed.) (1994) *Gendering Welfare States*, London, Sage.

Sainsbury, D. (ed.) (1999) *Gender and Welfare State Regimes*, Oxford, Oxford University Press.

Sevenhuijsen, S. (2000) 'Caring in the third way: the relation between obligation, responsibility and care in *Third Way* discourse', *Critical Social Policy*, vol.20, no.1, pp.5–38.

Shakespeare, T. (2000) 'The social relations of care' in Lewis et al. (eds) (2000).

Shildrick, M. (2004) 'Silencing sexuality: the regulation of the disabled body' in Carabine (ed.) (2004).

Silva, E.B. (1999) 'Transforming housewifery: dispositions, practices and technologies' in Silva, E.B. and Smart, C. (eds) *The New Family?*, London, Sage.

Spock, B. (1946) *Baby and Child Care*, New York, Duell, Sloan and Pearce.

Stone, D. (2000) 'Caring by the book' in Meyer, M.H. (ed.) *Care Work: Gender, Labour and the Welfare State*, London, Routledge.

Townsend, P. (1957) *The Family Life of Old People*, London, Routledge and Kegan Paul.

Townsend, P. (1959) Unpublished diary, File 10, Box 37, *The Peter Townsend Collection*, National Social Policy and Social Change Archive, Albert Sloman Library, University of Essex.

Tronto, J. (1993) *Moral Boundaries. A Political Argument for an Ethic of Care*, London, Routledge.

Twigg, J. (2000) *Bathing – The Body and Community Care*, London, Routledge.

Twigg, J. and Atkin, K. (1994) *Carers Perceived: Policy and Practice in Informal Care*, Buckingham, Open University Press.

Ungerson, C. (1983) 'Women and caring: skills, tasks and taboos' in Gamarnikow, D., Morgan, D., Purvis, J. and Taylorson, D. (eds) *The Public and the Private*, London, Heinemann.

Ungerson, C. (1987) *Policy is Personal: Sex, Gender and Informal Care*, London, Tavistock.

Webster, W. (1998) *Imagining Home: Gender, 'Race' and National Identity 1945–64*, London, UCL Press.

Weeks, J., Heaphy, B. and Donovan, C. (2001) *Same Sex Intimacies: Families of Choice and Other Life Experiments*, London, Routledge.

Widdowson, E. (2004) 'Retiring lives? Old age, work and welfare' in Mooney (ed.) (2004).

Williams, F. (2000) 'Principles of recognition and respect in welfare' in Lewis et al. (eds) (2000).

Williams, F. (2001) 'In and beyond New Labour: towards a new political ethics of care', *Critical Social Policy*, vol.21, no.4, pp.467–93.

CHAPTER 2

Personal Costs and Personal Pleasures: Care and the Unmarried Woman in Inter-War Britain

By Katherine Holden

Contents

1   Introduction

During the first half of the twentieth century a large amount of the physical care of children, older people and those who were sick was undertaken by unmarried women. They were widely employed in institutions as teachers, nurses, matrons and house mothers, and in middle- and upper-class homes as nannies and domestic servants. As maternity nurses, health visitors and social workers, they assisted and advised mothers, often becoming acknowledged experts in baby and child care. As sisters, daughters, aunts and family friends, they were involved in a range of long- and short-term informal, and usually unpaid, care arrangements, looking after sick or older relatives and fostering children when parents were dead, ill or abroad. The availability of unmarried women to undertake caring work had major implications for the development of welfare services and the emerging welfare state in the mid twentieth century; their labour power constituted an important but often unrecognized resource both for families and the state. But equally importantly, expectations that they should become carers helped to shape and had a special significance for the personal lives of women who never married.

It is this category of women and the personal costs and pleasures of their care relations that are the main subject of this chapter. Looking at a group of carers distant from us in time allows us to identify some of the factors that influence the way in which care is socially constructed in a particular historical moment, and casts new light on our own assumptions about the way in which care is organized today. The inter-war years have been chosen because this was a time of significant demographic change, of expanding welfare provision on the cusp of the post-war welfare state and of increased, although by the standards of the UK today, circumscribed, work opportunities for unmarried women. We ask what prompted unmarried women to become carers and examine contexts in which they gave care, the meanings that were attached to their caring activities and the kind of caring identities created by and for them.

Our analysis is focused upon the relationship between ideas about care, the material conditions in which care was provided and the personal lives of women who became carers. This is not a simple relationship. People make sense of their own experiences from a range of ideas and imagery within their culture, which determine what they may or may not say, and, looking back on their lives with hindsight, often see things from new perspectives (Waters, 2000).

In the inter-war years, unmarried women carers were sometimes idealized, as illustrated in Figures 2.1 and 2.2, offering practical support to their families or love and care for motherless children. But they were also demonized as 'busybodies' and seen to be interfering in the lives of families or neglecting children in orphanages. Such polarized images are still used to describe past generations of unmarried women carers, but as you will see, the stories the women themselves tell suggest that their lived experiences were more complex and multi-dimensional.

The focus of the chapter requires us to scrutinize a number of the concepts introduced in Chapter 1 to explain why people become carers. These range

Photo by Lambert Weston, Folkestone.

Figure 2.1   'Ministering angels' at the Damer Dawson Memorial Home

Figure 2.2   'No life of her own' from the *Woman's Friend*, 15 January 1938

from love, duty, obligation, attachment and reciprocity, to emotional need and financial necessity. Analysing these concepts helps us to see how care unsettles the boundaries of paid and unpaid work. The difficulties many unmarried women had in making clear-cut distinctions between 'caring for' and 'caring about' become more comprehensible and so also do contradictions between beliefs that caring should be a labour of love, that the state should provide care for its citizens and that caring work should be given a monetary value.

For unmarried women in the inter-war years the instability of the boundaries of paid and unpaid work created particular difficulties. Most married women gave up or were barred from paid work and their unpaid work within the family was financed by husbands whose pay scales were set at levels which were supposed to support a family. Rates of pay for women were much lower, yet those who remained unmarried were often expected by their families and by the state both to provide unpaid care *and* to contribute financially to their parents' support. Such anomalies were largely ignored by employers and by the state: women's wages and unemployment benefit were set at rates which assumed they had no dependants.

Yet, despite their anomalous position, few unmarried women looking back on their lives saw their marital status as a problem in relation to care. For many, being a carer provided a rationale for why they had not married, while not being married offered an explanation as to why they were carers – both within and outside the family.

Aims   The aims, then, of this chapter are to:

- Explore how ideas about gender, class, 'race', age and marital status interacted to produce particular constructions of care in the inter-war years.

- Examine the effects of demographic change, political and economic opportunities and social and cultural beliefs and expectations on unmarried women's availability and willingness to care.

- Consider the ways in which inter-war social policies and unmarried women's personal experiences (their choices, decisions and restraints in areas such as lifestyle, work and employment status) were mutually constitutive.

The chapter examines sources from (or relating to) the inter-war years, suggests how they can be used as research evidence and draws upon current ideas and approaches to care. The main sources are:

- stories and illustrations from books, magazines and newspapers dating from the inter-war years;

- extracts from oral history interviews with women who never married or married late in life;

- statistical data from the 1921 and 1931 census.

We question the meanings attached to being an unmarried female carer in these sources and their relative value in showing different perspectives on care. How, for example, can we make sense of the range of often conflicting representations of unmarried women carers, as brave and heroic, interfering, or dutiful? What value do census statistics have in counting 'surplus' women and women employed in caring occupations? What do they obscure? And, how far can oral history, which requires women to look back on their lives with hindsight from a present-day perspective, illuminate the complexities of and tensions within unmarried women's caring identities in the past?

The discussion draws upon feminist theories which suggest how the feminine norms of love, duty and reciprocity have worked together to construct unmarried women's caring identities. It also uses the psychoanalytic concepts of 'sublimation', 'splitting' and 'projection' (these terms are defined later) in order to illuminate our analysis of the conflicts and tensions around care in the personal lives of unmarried women. Looking at research evidence through these analytic lenses also helps us see why women carers in the inter-war years were often represented as either ministering angels or frustrated, uncaring old maids, and enables us to relate these representations to the material contexts in which care was given and received in this period. Such an approach draws upon a concept of 'the personal' which emphasizes the ways in which individuals during their life course may conform on some levels to normative expectations of themselves as gendered and 'racialized' welfare subjects but, at the same time, find ways of actively shaping, resisting and subverting these expectations.

2   Why is marital status important?

We begin by looking at the significance of marital status for women. As Joan Chandler (1991, p.2) has argued, marriage is a dominant institution in our society whose 'structure and ideology are central to the gendering of women'.

institution of marriage The **institution of marriage** casts its shadow over all women, who are routinely judged in terms of their relationship to it. But in order to analyse how marital categories work in relation to care, it is important to distinguish 'unmarried women' – defined in this chapter as those who have never been married and never had children – within the broader categorization 'single'. The term 'single' is unsatisfactory for our analysis because it includes other groups, such as divorcees, widows and lone mothers, who are often conflated on the grounds that they are all 'not married', ignoring thereby the divergent assumptions and imagery attached to them.

Age is also an important factor. In the inter-war years, singleness for women in their teens and early twenties was regarded as a 'natural' state leading up to marriage and was often associated with the terms 'bachelor girl' and 'flapper', used in the 1920s to signify youth, freedom and irresponsibility. However, for women aged over 30, singleness was more negatively perceived and could signify abnormality and deviance. Some of the most powerful imagery in this respect has been associated with the terms 'spinster' and 'old maid', deemed politically incorrect today but which still demean unmarried women.

Negative stereotypes of spinsterhood were common in the early and mid twentieth century, positioning older women who had never married as inferior and disadvantaged, outside the boundaries of acceptable femininity by virtue of their age, physical appearance, asexuality (or deviant sexuality) and childlessness. As Stuart Hall has argued, such stereotyping 'facilitates the "binding" or bonding of all of Us who are normal into one "imagined community" and it sends into symbolic exile all of Them – "the Others" – who are different' (Hall, 1997, quoted in Walter, 2001, p.22). Excluded from the imagined community of marriage and frequently characterized as marginal within families, spinsters were mocked as pathetic, lonely, sexually frustrated, or masculine figures. Such representations often had a dual message, showing older unmarried women as envious of or aspiring unsuccessfully to be like married women. Thus, spinsters who had failed in the marriage market were often shown to have failed in other areas of their lives. The following passage from a children's story *The Children who Lived in a Barn*, written by Eleanor Graham (1896–1984), founder of Puffin books, and first published in 1938, illustrates this point:

> Miss Ruddle, the district visitor, or DV for short, was one of those people who always seem to be saying: *Don't come near me with those dirty hands!* She was thin and sharp featured and of a most interfering nature. The villagers hated her, for she poked her nose inside their cottages and tried to discover things that were nothing whatsoever to do with her. She had a passion for 'showing them how'. She showed them how to keep house, how to look after their children, how to cook, how to save money, how to spend their money (which was worse), how to look after their husbands, how to manage so that they could go to church on Sunday morning – in fact there was no end to the things she showed them.
>
> (Graham, 1965, p.54)

What stereotypes do you think are being reproduced here and how do they work to discredit Miss Ruddle's authority as an expert in domestic and caring work?

This passage positions women who are wives and mothers as the 'natural' carers. The family is cast as a private caring world in which the outsider Miss Ruddle (the district visitor who represents the uncaring state) had no right to interfere. The message is reinforced by giving her attributes which are the antithesis of the loving wife and mother – she is thin, sharp and intolerant, and keeps people at a distance. They define her status as a woman who has 'missed out' on the primary experiences of womanhood and whose professional expertise in housewifery and child care can thus be devalued and ignored. Attacks of this kind were also directed at women teachers who were regularly accused of being 'withered' or 'jaundiced' spinsters or sexual inverts (lesbians), unsuitable to take charge of young children (Oram, 1989). Such constructions also implicitly and sometimes explicitly make assumptions about unmarried women's personal lives as unfulfilled and abnormal.

Were any of these stereotypes applied to teachers or welfare workers in your childhood? If so, what assumptions were made about their marital status? Do you have any more positive memories of unmarried women: for example, of an aunt, a godmother or a teacher?

There is considerable evidence that such stereotypes were often challenged or ignored. Many unmarried women were much loved by their families and communities and valued for the care they gave, and they were also important figures in developing policy in areas such as health services, child welfare and social work. We explore this paradox in the rest of the chapter; we consider why such contradictory visions of the unmarried woman have been held in British culture and what effects they had on the creation of identity for the women themselves.

3   Policy contexts: normative belief systems, material conditions and employment trends

This section will map ideas about gender, 'race' and demography in relation to unmarried women and examine the impact of these ideas on economic and welfare policies in the inter-war years. This provides further contexts for spinster stereotypes and offers ways of understanding why so many unmarried women became carers, both in the home and in the community.

3.1   Gender, marital status and sublimation

Our first task is to consider why unmarried women were encouraged to do caring work in the inter-war years, a question which necessitates looking more closely at how gender and marital status interacted to produce particular constructions of womanhood in this period. Feminist theorists have suggested that the 'decision to care is made within a framework of widely held assumptions that caring is women's work and that in the end caring should take precedence over other types of work' (Lewis and Meredith, 1988, p.5). In the inter-war years the expectation that a woman's 'natural' work was to be a wife, providing sexual services for her husband and caring for her family, was much stronger than it is today. But, at the same time, the importance of both sexual and maternal fulfilment for women within marriage was widely publicized in marriage manuals such as the best-selling book *Married Love*, by the birth control pioneer Marie Stopes (1918). The tensions between these two sets of expectations which demanded that women must satisfy both their own and their family's needs were not always reconcilable. Such conflicts often

unconscious anxieties

resulted in **unconscious anxieties**: married women's failure to live up to these ideals could be denied and attached to unmarried women who were frequently believed to be unfulfilled and frustrated. This was one reason why unpaid work in child care, domestic work or nursing was so frequently recommended to help unmarried women retain their feminine 'nature' and compensate them for not being married.

Psychologists in Britain, influenced by the sexologist Havelock Ellis and the psychoanalytic theories of Sigmund Freud, took up this idea. They believed that the repression or denial of unmarried women's sexual and maternal instincts might lead to neurosis or sexual inversion (lesbianism) unless these

sublimation

instincts were sublimated. **Sublimation** was believed to be an unconscious process by which sexual instincts were diverted from their original ends (sexual activity and reproduction) and redirected to non-sexual purposes. The redirection of sexual instincts into non-sexual activities also meant that the idea of sublimation carried with it a social element, in the sense that sublimated activities were regarded as socially acceptable or, as one psychologist described them, 'satisfying to the individual and of value to the community' (Hadfield, 1924, quoted in Oram, 1992). Caring work, particularly with mothers and children, was recommended therefore as being a particularly satisfying social activity.

ACTIVITY 2.1

Read the passages from Marie Stopes's private correspondence, reproduced in Extracts 2.1 and 2.2 below.

■   What personal and social policy agendas in relation to unmarried women, 'race' and class can you discern here?

■   In what ways do the writers implicitly draw upon the concept of sublimation?

Extract 2.1 is part of a letter from Stopes to a man who believed his sister had no prospect of ever getting married because she had a minor disability. In Extract 2.2 the two passages were written by a 30-year-old unmarried midwife, Miss E, in letters to Stopes.

Extract 2.1   Marie Stopes and sublimation

Sometimes if it is explained to them that by serving the community in some such way as a nurse to children or hospital nurse they are really doing for the [British] race work equivalent to the natural production of children, they may take it up wholeheartedly and find moral satisfaction in it. I know of a good many women who were sex hungry who have satisfied it by being maternity nurses.

(Marie Stopes Papers, 1920, MCS to WJH, PP/MCS/A132)

Extract 2.2   Miss E and sublimation

I am now reduced to earning my own living, after having a very liberal allowance in years gone by, and as I have a little adopted girl to keep, I am obliged to earn a good £150 a year to make ends meet. My baby is nearly 5, her name is Marie and she was a little unwanted atom weighing 2lbs 6oz. I looked after her from birth in hospital in 1916, and when her mother said she was going to let her die because she did not want her, I nearly broke my heart. I vowed that I would keep her. She is now such a sweet child growing up under the care of a dear old lady in Hampshire. That is my little contribution toward loving Humanity and how proud I am to work for that wee mite.

...

Do you know, much as I long to be loved by a good, fine man – I am beginning to see that my life is the happiest. I am tending all day long the mothers and babies (work I adore) and in addition to that, there are channels innumerable into which I can pour the abundance of love and affection I have stored inside me.

(Marie Stopes Papers, 1921, KE to MCS, PP/MCS/A78)

COMMENT

Stopes makes the assumption that caring is woman's work but she is also addressing directly the vexed issue of unmarried women's feelings and desires. She suggests that sexual energy (termed 'sex hunger') can be satisfied (or sublimated) through work and, like many doctors and psychologists, she thought this should be maternally oriented. But her description of maternity nursing as 'race work' also has another agenda. In sympathy with the aims of the Eugenics Society (**Carabine, 2004a; Doolittle, 2004**), which believed that unhealthy mothers would pass on a hereditary weakness to their children and that only the fittest should be allowed to bear children, Stopes regarded improving the health of children and enabling women to have healthy babies as of crucial importance to the British race. It was a task she thought well-suited to unmarried women who could not, or (in this case) should not, have children of their own.

care chain

The midwife, Miss E, had been jilted by her fiancé and stressed to Stopes in earlier letters how strongly she had been influenced by *Married Love* and her later book *Radiant Motherhood* (1920). Miss E found the idea that she was sublimating her sexual and maternal energy into work with mothers and children helpful, but also believed that in adopting an unwanted child she was contributing to a wider good. However, as a single working mother, Miss E could not care for the child herself and had her fostered. We can therefore also see evidence of a **care chain** here similar to that conceptualized by Hochschild (see Chapter 1). In this period, child adoption was not legalized or regulated by the state and it was not uncommon for British middle-class unmarried women to adopt babies and to use other women of other classes or ethnicities to care for them. The conflicts that arose in this kind of care work will be discussed below.

3.2   White woman's mission: unmarried women and 'race'

Another way in which middle-class unmarried women created caring identities was by becoming missionaries and, even if this was not realized in practice, dreams of missionary work abroad could still influence women's perceptions of themselves as carers. Going abroad in reality and fantasy allowed an escape from the safety and confinement of 'home', and unmarried women often drew upon ideas about Empire and of Britain as the 'Motherland' to construct white, maternal, Christian identities which enabled them to assert moral authority over women and children of other ethnicities and faiths (Ware, 1992). In so doing, they were using the Victorian idea of 'woman's mission to woman' which had justified middle-class women leaving the home to rescue and care for 'fallen women' in the inner cities on the grounds of their common sisterhood.

However, in the context of Empire, the idea of 'woman's mission' was also linked to theories of 'racial' and religious difference which validated white women's superior knowledge, and positioned other faiths and cultures as dirty, uncivilized and inferior and women of colour as victims or childlike dependants. For example, the Girls' Friendly Society (GFS), a religious organization set up in the 1870s to save working-class girls from 'falling', supported women missionaries in Africa, Japan, China and India, most of whom were unmarried. These missionaries undertook caring work in hospitals and schools but their main goal was to convert the 'natives' to Christianity and educate them into the manners, habits and dispositions of white femininity.

ACTIVITY 2.2

Read Extract 2.3 from *Friendship's Highway*, a history of the Girls' Friendly Society written by an unmarried member of the GFS, Miss Mary Heath-Stubbs, in 1935. The missionary it describes is shown in Figure 2.3.

- What kinds of caring identities are being constructed in the picture and text?
- How do they position women and children as 'racialized' subjects?

Extract 2.3   The white woman's mission in Zanzibar

In Zanzibar the Society has its own Missionary, Miss Bridges Lee, working under the U.M.C.A. Her chief work is done among children, visiting schools in Zanzibar and in the neighbourhood. How happy these little Christian children are in the schools may be guessed from the fact that during an epidemic of chicken pox Miss Bridges Lee was kept busy 'shooing spotty babies away.' 'They will come, they love school so.' But her influence extends far beyond children ... No wonder that Miss Lee concludes 'It is indeed a wonderful privilege to be allowed to share in this work of leading the African people to our Lord.'

(Heath-Stubbs, 1935, p.85)

COMMENT

The text describes one missionary's personal dedication to her work but also shows her and the author's sense of superiority as white women. For the GFS, whiteness was a quality associated with Christianity, purity and being British. The author uses the missionary's status as a white woman implicitly in this passage to position people in Zanzibar as passive recipients of care and education. These ideas are reinforced in the text, where children are described as coming to school even when they are ill, and in Figure 2.3, which shows the missionary joining hands with her class of African children. We can also get a sense in the text of the personal pleasures white women missionaries could gain from African people's conversion to Christianity and from the love the 'spotty babies' offered their teacher. Psychologists at this time would have interpreted this as sublimation, but Miss Lee's position as an unmarried woman in Britain also left her vulnerable to being classified as 'Other'. In Africa it may have been easier for her to break free of the spinster stereotype because of her identity, status and social position as a white, British woman.

Figure 2.3   GFS missionary with her scholars in Zanzibar

Heath-Stubbs's promotion of white women's missionary work is also suggestive of her anxieties about the potency of the British race. As anthropologist Mary Douglas (1991, p.3) suggests, in all societies 'certain moral values are upheld and certain social rules defined by beliefs in dangerous contagion'. At a time when Britain's birth rate was in decline and its hold on Empire precarious, it was important that the 'Motherland' should not be contaminated by other 'races' and cultures. White women were needed to model British values of domesticity and Christianity. In this respect, the caring and missionary work offered by older women, who, by not marrying, had **gatekeeping**   themselves transgressed social norms, can be viewed as **gatekeeping**. In their quest for social and sexual purity, which they describe as 'white', they were managing the boundary between order and chaos both at home and abroad. This sense of Britain, and specifically of England, as a white Christian fortress under siege can be seen in the launch by the GFS of a Great White Crusade in 1920 as a part of the 'great struggle against impurity' on the grounds that 'the only way to keep England white is to keep it in touch with God' (Heath-Stubbs, 1935, p.111).

3.3   'Surplus' women and emigration

Middle-class unmarried women's desire to do caring and missionary work must also be related to an ongoing debate during the nineteenth and early twentieth centuries about the 'redundancy' of single women, who were perceived to be 'surplus' to the needs of the nation and encouraged to emigrate to the Empire in search of new opportunities and marriage prospects. This debate was renewed after the First World War when, fuelled by the publication of the 1921 census statistics, the 'problems' resulting from an imbalance of the sexes were linked to the idea of a 'lost generation' of men and widely reported in the press. Figures showed that the 'excess' of women had reached the unprecedented heights of 1,096 females per thousand males, prompting renewed suggestions that women should emigrate to find work and husbands.

Feminist historians have shown how the surplus woman debate was also linked to eugenic concerns about the falling birth rate and the failure of middle-class spinsters of healthy stock to become mothers (Jeffreys, 1985; Oram, 1992; **Doolittle, 2004**). The significance of this failure was underlined by reports of the poor health of the nation's children and, as we shall see, this had important policy implications for the development of child welfare services in which unmarried women were to play such a key role.

While in the (white) Dominions (Australia, New Zealand, Canada, Rhodesia and South Africa) there was equal concern that unmarried women emigrants should be of good hereditary stock, they were not looking for missionaries, teachers or nurses, but rather for 'healthy, wholesome British domestic girls ... of the right type' (Gothard, 1990, p.72) to go into service. This also fitted with the aims of the Overseas Settlement Committee, the British government body established in 1919 to deal with Empire migration, whose objective was to populate the Dominions with 'new settlers, British by birth and British in sympathies' (Gothard, 1990, p.80). Only those women willing to consider domestic work, whatever their class background, were encouraged to emigrate. So great was the demand that, in the late 1920s, training centres were set up for British women, jointly funded by the British, Australian and Canadian governments, giving instruction in cooking, laundry, care of the house and needlework, and their passage was paid for by the country of arrival. Governesses and nurses were also expected to do housework in addition to their professional duties. However, it is clear that the interests and aspirations of unmarried women themselves did not always fit with the policies outlined above and the number of women willing to commit themselves to this kind of work, both in Britain and abroad, was far lower than the demand.

3.4 Conceptualizing women's work: marriage, motherhood and service

To understand the conflicts that could arise between government policy in relation to domestic work and women's own desires and ambitions, we need to consider why care and women's paid work were so closely identified with one another. This necessitates returning to the dominant image of the wife and mother which overshadowed other representations of womanhood in this period. Women's work within marriage has been perceived as having no market value, performed not for financial motives but out of love and duty and in response to the needs of family (collapsing the distinction between caring for and caring about). As a result, work for all women, married or not, assumed the primacy of a service role in which financial remuneration and individual satisfaction were regarded as secondary considerations. These assumptions and expectations had major implications for the personal lives of all women, making it more difficult for them to value their work in other terms and by other standards.

This had two consequences for unmarried women. First, caring and service occupations were assumed to be the most suitable and 'natural' forms of paid work; and, second, low pay scales for this work were regarded as justifiable by the government, employers and trade unions. Since most women were assumed to be working not just for themselves but as part of a family unit, their wages were regarded as supplementary to those of a male family breadwinner and those who remained living with their families were classed as their parents' dependants. Yet many working-class unmarried women in these occupations had little choice but to remain, not dependent on their **financially** families, but **financially interdependent** with them. Social surveys and oral **interdependent** histories of the inter-war years show that the wage-earning power of adult unmarried daughters (even those in low-paid care work) was essential in many working-class families to keep them above the poverty line. These sources also show that some unmarried women in such situations had difficulty in surviving on their own.

3.5   Unmarried women's paid work: 'the servant problem'

As in the Dominions, the biggest demand for women's work in Britain in the inter-war years was in personal service, which accounted for roughly a third of all employed women. This category was broadly conceived within the 1931 census to include nannies and nursery nurses, servants in clubs and hotels and care workers in institutions for homeless children and sick, disabled or older people. The census showed 23 per cent of occupied (employed) women as domestic servants (Taylor, 1979), but only one servant in twelve was married and half a million (47.5 per cent) were over 30, which suggests the increasing reluctance of younger women to enter service when other employment opportunities existed. Older unmarried women were often obliged to enter service after leaving other employment such as shop or office work, in which there were expectations that workers should be young, attractive and compliant. It is also likely that fewer domestic service workers left to get married than those in other occupations, given the restrictions imposed upon their daily lives, such as anti-social hours, limited social interactions and the discouragement of male 'followers'. Yet, despite the fact that many women were forced into domestic service jobs, demand consistently outstripped supply, contributing to what was commonly termed 'the servant problem'.

These statistics do not, however, include all women in the categories of personal and domestic service. Many others took on casual work which was not counted or where they received payment in kind for caring services. Neither do statistical returns tell us much about the policy interests or individual costs and benefits for the various interested parties, including the government, employers, families and the women themselves. For these we need to turn to other kinds of research evidence.

From the government standpoint, the 'servant problem' was connected to the refusal of many unmarried women to enter domestic service after they had been discharged at the end of the First World War from more lucrative work in factories or offices to make way for decommissioned servicemen. To address this 'problem', a number of policies were instigated: the only training offered to unemployed women was in homecraft, grants were given to purchase servants' uniforms and unemployment benefit was refused to women who would not take domestic service jobs. Examples of this kind illustrate some of the ways in which social policy has been used to attempt (not always successfully) to shape the content of workers' personal lives.

Two government investigations, *The Report of the Women's Advisory Committee of the Ministry of Reconstruction on the Domestic Service Problem* (1919) and *The Report to the Ministry of Labour of the Committee to Enquire into the Conditions as to the supply of Female Domestic Servants* (1923), also tried to remedy the situation by recommending better training conditions and a higher status for servants but their advice was never implemented (Beddoe, 1989, p.63).

Why do you think this was the case? Think back to our more general discussions of the status of care and service in relation to women's work.

Middle-class housewives saw themselves as the main victims of the 'servant problem' which became a major issue in the inter-war years. The difficulty of getting and keeping good servants, their refusal to know their place, their idiosyncrasies and rivalries and their tendency to leave without notice to look for a better position were frequent topics of discussion and often satirized in women's fiction and magazines. The heat generated from this debate illustrates conflicts between the interests and needs of women in different class positions and with unequal access to power.

ACTIVITY 2.3

Study the cartoons in Figures 2.4(a) and 2.4(b) taken from *Good Housekeeping* (April 1933).

■   What is their main message?

■   What conflicts are portrayed?

Try linking them to the social policies being promoted in relation to domestic service at this time and the responses of unmarried women being coerced into these jobs.

COMMENT

The first picture portrays a mistress being intimidated by the cook she is interviewing while in the second she is at the mercy of quarrelling servants. While married, middle-class women were in the more powerful employer position, such images reflect the anxieties of women who were themselves 'kept' by their husbands. Women in this position often felt they had little control over unmarried servants who might choose not to take jobs offered and might leave at any time without notice.

"Her qualifications were unimpeachable, her appearance formidable"

Figure 2.4(a) 'The anxious and intimidated interviewer'

Figure 2.4(b) 'When the war inevitably blazes out in the open, the mistress is forced to arbitrate'

The parents of women going into domestic service had differing views of this kind of employment. While some were keen for their daughters to gain more lucrative jobs, others saw service as the safest and most desirable option, which also offered them a potential training ground for marriage. The oral historian Pam Taylor's interview with Jenny Owen, one of five sisters in Wales who went into service in London, suggests that the interdependence of unmarried daughters and their families could be highly valued:

> We had money in our pockets then ... And we sent [home] nearly half our wages – not in money but in things that were needed. And through us all in service we practically furnished my mother's home and the bedding ... Well my father said more than once he would prefer to have twelve girls again than two boys, we'd done so much for them.

(Taylor, 1979, p.130)

This idealized memory comes from a Welsh woman who had left a mining district which had high levels of unemployment. While it is revealing about the gendered nature of domestic service, it tells us little about the private costs and conflicts, including heavy physical work and high levels of surveillance. There is also no sense here of the reluctance of many unmarried women in cities to conform to prescribed gendered expectations by going into service, highlighted in newspaper reports immediately after the First World War. For example, in December 1918 *The Daily Telegraph* claimed that at one labour exchange only one woman out of 3,000 entered her name as willing to go into service (Beddoe, 1989, p.51).

3.6   Migration, Empire and 'the servant problem'

One reason for the high numbers of women still in personal and domestic service in the 1920s was the availability of Irish migrant labour. Unmarried women, particularly in rural districts of Ireland with high female unemployment, had poorer marriage and job prospects in their home country than they had in Britain. Two thirds of the population between 1880 and 1920 never married and many women left to find work abroad, some having been trained for emigration by staying in school longer and acquiring the literacy needed for employment in urban environments abroad (Nolan, 1989). In 1920, 85 per cent of women migrants aged 15 to 35 were unmarried and many went into the jobs rejected by British women – while Irish servants were perceived as lower in the 'racial' and class hierarchy, they were also believed to be more compliant and hardworking. Oral history interviews with women who had been in domestic service in the 1930s suggest that employers were 'really anxious for Irish girls because they were strong and they'd do the work' (Lennon et al., 1988, p.42).

Thus despite their whiteness, which meant they were distinguishable from the British only by their accent and perhaps their name, Irish unmarried women in personal and domestic service were often employed to do rough, dirty work and they faced discrimination. This was in contrast to British servants in the Dominions whose whiteness and Britishness was an advantage. Irish servants who 'lived-in' in middle-class households were more isolated and less likely to be the victims of direct discrimination, but often took longer to acclimatize to British working-class communities than those in personal service jobs, such as pub work or waitressing, who had the support of other migrant workers (Walter, 2001). The following quotation exposes the levels of economic hardship, racist prejudice and loneliness suffered by Irish women in personal service occupations, but also their sense of solidarity:

> In the thirties things were really bad here. You'd go after a room and they'd say 'Don't take Irish'. I got into Joe Lyons as a nippy (waitress). You had to be nippy and all. The Irish helped each other out. You'd let them share your bed until they got on their feet. Some of the girls I knew cried a lot. They wanted to go back home but they couldn't. The work the English girls wouldn't do, the Irish did.
>
> (Lennon and Lennon, 1980, quoted in Walter, 2001, p.147)

ACTIVITY 2.4

The newspaper extract given below formed part of a correspondence in *The Times*, and was written in response to a leading article entitled 'Surplus women' published two weeks earlier on 25 August 1921.

■   What economic, class and 'racial' agendas are contained within it and how would they have influenced the personal lives of unmarried women?

■   Compare this with the reception given to Irish women going into domestic service in Britain.

WOMEN IN THE MAJORITY.
AN IMPERIAL PROBLEM.

DOMESTIC WORK AND EMIGRATION.

... In many parts of the Dominions even the immigration of men is not meeting with encouragement; while the influx of a large number of women into the various branches of industrial and professional life would be resisted to the death. In order to guard against this

last possibility the Dominions have set up their own organization for dealing with the immigration of women from this country, and have made it very clear that there is one type of woman, and only one, whom they will welcome in large numbers and to whom they will give financial and other help. This is the woman willing to do domestic work.

(*The Times*, 5 September 1921, p.9)

COMMENT

Demand for domestic servants in the Dominions was similar to that in the 'home country', but the lure of 'abroad' encouraged some women who would not normally have considered going into service to take a risk. The financial assistance offered gave them the chance of a more adventurous life, a new source of work and potential marriage partners.

However, while the British and Dominion governments were anxious to increase the numbers of families of British stock in the Empire, their interest was only in white domesticated women 'of the right type' who 'could help in the home as a first step towards entering a home of her own' (Gothard, 1990, p.80). Although white Irish women migrants may have had similar hopes for better work and marriage prospects, and demand for servants in Britain was equally high, they were in a different position. The troubled relations between the two countries made the integration of Irish communities in Britain more problematic. The Irish were 'Other' and associated with dirt and disorder. Thus despite their common whiteness and marital status, unmarried Irish servants in Britain were more likely to face discrimination on grounds of ethnicity than were British servants in the Dominions.

3.7   Unmarried women's paid work: the caring professions

As Figure 2.5 illustrates, care and service work for middle-class unmarried women had a very different status from that of domestic service. Some women saw the caring professions as an escape from the stifling confinement of the home, offering financial independence, emotional satisfaction and service to others. Their increasing movement into paid positions in welfare services in the inter-war years was also an extension of their earlier involvement in philanthropic or charitable voluntary work, and was facilitated by a number of important policy developments. These were: the Sex Disqualification Removal Act 1919, allowing the entry of women into all the professions except the Civil Service; the professionalization of midwifery, health visiting, nursing and social work; the establishment of a Ministry of Health in 1919; and the growth of state maternal and child welfare services following the Maternity and Child Welfare Act 1918.

The expertise claimed by unmarried women employed in these services often involved instructing or advising other women in household management, health and child care. While pay scales were substantially lower than in male-oriented professions, unmarried women in professional caring roles were able to seek parity with and demonstrate superiority over married women, showing their skills as homemakers without needing a husband. Marriage bars, antisocial hours and beliefs about the centrality of the male breadwinner during the 1920s and 1930s meant that few of these positions were filled by married women.

We saw in section 2 (in the case of Miss Ruddle) how spinster stereotypes could be employed to discredit women in this position. The following passage shows how the surplus woman debate and the idea of sublimation could be harnessed positively to validate the work unmarried women were doing in the caring professions.

Figure 2.5   A London County Council committee volunteer visiting in Deptford, 1939

ACTIVITY 2.5

The passage given in Extract 2.4, from a biography of the social work pioneer, Geraldine Aves, describes an incident during her education at Cambridge University in 1920.

- How might it have affected Aves's choice of career?
- What feminine expectations are being reinforced here?
- Can you see any hidden agenda?

Extract 2.4   Geraldine Aves and sublimation

It was during her last year at Newnham that a distinguished woman doctor came to give a lecture on the subject of the relationship between men and women, and the ways in which they normally sought to attract one another. Well aware that, for her generation, potential husbands had during the war years been decimated, Geraldine listened attentively: 'The thing that deeply impressed me was her description of how young women had to face the fact that many of them would not get married. She talked about sublimation and how you can, in fact, have a very well worth-while, interesting and happy life if you somehow adjust to that'. It helped Geraldine come to accept that, although she liked the company of men very much, and got on well with them, she could do without them.

(Willmott, 1992, p.28)

COMMENT

Aves's biographer tells a story which can also be found in other biographies, autobiographies and oral histories of women from a similar age cohort. It suggests that educated young women immediately after the war were being encouraged to sublimate sexual and maternal desires, not to assume that they would marry and to direct their energies elsewhere. This advice may have influenced Aves in making her career choice to engage in social work with children. During the inter-war years, she was appointed on to the School Care Committee of the London County Council's Education Department and co-ordinated part of the evacuation programme at the start of the Second World War. However, biographies and autobiographies are always written with hindsight. The concept of sublimation and the idea of a lost generation also offered Willmott, and Aves herself, a *post hoc* explanation for her lack of a husband, her work with children and her close emotional attachments to women. By describing the incident in this way, Aves's personal relationships, both through her work and in her private life, could be viewed by readers as substitutes for marriage rather than choices in their own right.

3.8   Unmarried women's caring work in the home

Not all unmarried women's caring work lay within the boundaries of paid employment. Working mothers, or those who had gone abroad with their husbands, often relied on the services of unmarried female family members and/or friends to care for their children. Where parents had died or were unable to care for their children, long-term fostering and informal adoption by unmarried women (as in the case of Miss E discussed in section 3.1) were also not uncommon, arrangements which could be legalized after the Adoption Act came into force in 1926.

Oral history interviews suggest strong expectations were also made of unmarried daughters to care for their parents in sickness and old age. Before any extensive network of state-funded nursing homes existed, older people who were sick or disabled and had no savings or relatives to support them often had to resort to public hospitals for care, many of which were still under the control of the much hated Poor Law Authorities. This had important implications for the personal lives of unmarried women. Their unpaid labour was regarded as an important material resource and some parents made a conscious decision to keep a daughter (usually the youngest) at home, discouraging her from marriage. The scarcity of self-contained accommodation and landladies' preferences for male lodgers also militated against unmarried daughters moving away from the family home.

There is little documentary evidence of how unmarried women negotiated the expectations and demands of their families. However, records of campaigning groups such as the Over Thirty Association and the National Spinsters' Pension Association (NSPA), which took up the cause of low paid older women workers, show the effects on employment prospects and social insurance provision of having to support elderly relatives. The NSPA, set up in 1935, was the largest women's reform movement of the 1930s, campaigning on behalf of older unmarried women workers who during the depression were losing their right to a contributory pension at 65 and were forced to rely on the means-tested public assistance or pension after the age of 70 (**Widdowson, 2004**). This usually happened because their insurance records were incomplete through unemployment, illness or giving up paid work to look after parents or other such 'home duties'. In 1938, the NSPA presented a petition to Parliament with nearly a million signatures demanding that spinsters should receive a state pension at the age of 55 on the same basis as widows, since many of them had dependants to support but were without the security of a husband's wage. While ultimately unsuccessful, it was influential in reducing the retirement age for all women from 65 to 60 in 1940. It is also significant historically as the first unmarried women's political group which recognized the financial implications of doing unpaid care for women's personal lives, and which was an active force in its lobbying for policy change, as Figure 2.6 illustrates.

Looking back on our introductory discussion, we can now see a range of interconnected beliefs, ideas and material conditions which between the two world wars shaped social policies and influenced the personal lives of women who never married. The emergence of the welfare state, the demand by families and institutions for paid and unpaid care, the high number of women in the population and the economic resources of women and their families are all important structural factors which militated in favour of unmarried women taking on caring work. But it has been equally important for us to recognize women's agency: the personal lives of unmarried women were not simply determined by material conditions, nor were they passive recipients of prevailing beliefs about spinsterhood or women's propensity to care. Rather, unmarried women negotiated these ideas and conditions, at times resisting them while at others helping to shape them in the context of both their personal lives and policy making. In the final part of this chapter, we go a step further in exploring these issues by linking normative belief systems and material conditions with psychic structures and unconscious processes in the lives of individual women.

Figure 2.6   Members of the National Spinsters' Pension Campaign London rally, 1937

4   Representing the personal lives of unmarried carers

In this section, we consider feminist and psychoanalytic perspectives on care and apply them to women's self-representation in oral history interviews. These interviews were undertaken for my doctoral thesis in the early 1990s (Holden, 1996), which explored the influence of the institution of marriage between the two world wars on the lives of women who never married. Rather than looking at them simply as evidence of particular life experiences, they are drawn upon here to show how caring identities could be created by women telling stories about their past lives. In analysing these stories, we ask what might be particularly important about those identities, identify tensions and instabilities inherent within them and show the conflicts which arose between care-givers, the recipients of care and carers' employers.

4.1   Feminist perspectives on care

Some of the feminist ideas on why women give care that we considered in Chapter 1 and earlier in this chapter are worth revisiting here, particularly the view that caring is a key component of a feminine identity. Gilligan (1982) argued that a feminine personality is characterized by a tendency to define itself primarily in relation to others, while Graham (1983) suggested the impossibility of divorcing the labour of tending from feelings of love and ties of obligation. Dalley (1988) saw this convergence as being rooted in 'the concentration of multiple functions of the role of the mother' who both bears and rears her child, but the fact women who have never borne children have also seen labour and love as entwined in the act of caring suggests that this social expectation is not only made of mothers. In their study of caring daughters, most of whom were single and childless, Lewis and Meredith (1988) found that the great majority saw caring as labour which they performed through ties of obligation, but that this usually rested on feelings of love and affection.

Finch's (1989) study of familial support gave much less credence to the part played by affection, looking rather at the significance of value systems. While she agreed that a sense of obligation and duty towards other family members is the most distinctive feature of kin relationships, for her this was not a matter of individual feelings or emotions but of morality based upon normative expectations. One of these expectations is **reciprocity** – a concept developed by anthropologists to explain why kin groups assist one another, based on the benefits they have received in the past or may receive from other members of the group in the future. The expectations of obligation built into parent–child relationships can be linked to a generalized societal view that children have a duty to support their parents because they have been supported by them. The concept of **duty** could also help to explain why so many unmarried daughters felt obliged to give their parents care when ties of affection were weak, even at the cost of renouncing other dreams or ambitions. It does not, however, explain why this expectation was made more frequently of daughters rather than sons and of unmarried rather than married daughters. We therefore need to look more closely at the gains and losses for individuals within this particular set of reciprocal relationships.

reciprocity

duty

4.2   Caring daughters: feminist perspectives

One route to exploring these theoretical positions is provided by my interview data. Using narratives from two participants who had renounced other desires and ambitions and had drawn upon the identity of caring daughter to tell their life histories, we consider how their motivations for adopting this identity show significant differences and illustrate the degree of complexity in caring identities.

Jane (born 1907, interviewed in 1990) had lived with her parents on a smallholding near Bristol and stressed how much she had loved outdoor work. Yet when in the late 1920s her parents returned to live in the city she trained to be a secretary primarily so that she could remain living at home rather than continuing to do farm work. Jane saw this as indicative of her very deep attachment to her mother rather than of any external pressure:

> I remember my mother saying, 'if you feel you want to leave home and get a flat and live on your own you can do it', but I didn't want to leave. I was very close to my mother. She was a wonderful mother to me. She was more than a wife and mother. She was an inspiration, I loved her so much. I think I worshipped the ground she walked on. I just didn't want to part. I could have done. I was free to as far as they were concerned.

A decade later Jane's decision not to marry and not to leave home proved to be of great significance to her family, when, during the Second World War, she gave up her paid job in order to care for her mother. Jane underlined the importance of this decision and the official backing she had received: 'I wasn't supposed to leave work because of the war effort. I said my mother was more important. I went to the ombudsman and got a certificate from my doctor saying it was essential for me to look after my mother and the ombudsman granted me leave immediately.'

Thus far, no conflicting claims or loyalties appear in Jane's story. She saw her caring work as a labour of love and 'the right thing to do', a reciprocal task performed because her mother had been so good to her. Yet by analysing other aspects of this life story, a more complex narrative emerges. Jane used her parents' need of her services as an explanation for having postponed marriage until she was in her fifties:

> My parents passed away before I was married. You see I couldn't ... well I knew this man, and he was living in The Hague. This might seem difficult to believe, but it's true. He wrote to me every day for eight years asking me to marry him. I couldn't because I was looking after my mother and it wouldn't have been fair to her or him.

Other interests were also at stake here which were not revealed in the formal interview. On an earlier occasion, while I was working for Jane as her cleaner, she told me that she had delayed her marriage to a widower with a young family because she did not want to be put into the position of being obliged to care for his children. This would not have been an easy role for Jane to reject after the Second World War when the British government was determined to rebuild families, and unmarried women were strongly encouraged to work with children and to care for motherless families. But Jane had not wanted children and the caring identity of loving, dutiful daughter was therefore useful to her in two respects. First, it offered her a rationale for refusing marriage at a time when she had other responsibilities, and second, it was a way of avoiding having to care for her fiancé's children, a task which, as their stepmother, she would have felt obligated to undertake. When Jane finally agreed to marry her suitor, her parents had died and his children were adults.

Doreen (born 1911, interviewed in 1993) also used the identity of a caring daughter as a reason not to have pursued other activities, but with very different motivations in mind. For her it was both a justification for not having pursued a more adventurous life path and a way of working out difficulties in her relationship with her father. Like Jane, Doreen had a farming background, but unusually her mother was in charge, employing her husband on the farm she had inherited and she had offered Doreen a model of female authority. As a child, Doreen had a difficult relationship with both her parents, suffering physical violence from her father and cold criticism from her mother. Her father's frustration at having to take orders from a woman may have been taken out on his daughter and he later made it difficult for her to have boyfriends.

In an attempt to escape the family, Doreen had tried unsuccessfully to persuade her parents to allow her to become a missionary, until one day she received a 'message from God':

> I knew 100 per cent from God that he didn't want me to be a missionary ... you do just know, and that at some stage I'd have my parents to look after. And that to me was the worst possible thing ... I wasn't in any doubt about it. He didn't want me to be a missionary. But he didn't leave me without a job, and that ultimately I would be responsible for my parents. And that I didn't want to accept at all because I just knew it was going to be very, very hard.

For Doreen, caring was not simply a labour of love but a 'woman's mission', a Christian duty which, as you saw earlier, was inspirational for so many unmarried women in the late nineteenth and early twentieth centuries. One interpretation of Doreen's dreams of being a missionary, therefore, is that they allowed her to create a strong moral authority and identity for herself as a carer which she could use as an alternative to marriage and motherhood.

The frustration of her dreams compelled Doreen to displace the white Christian missionary ideal on to the identity of the caring daughter, but she made it clear from her description of this task as 'the worst thing' that it was a duty rather than a labour of love. Her new mission was to look after her parents and, after her mother died, she took a job as a travelling farm secretary which allowed her to take work home so that she did not have to leave her father alone. Yet she also found a way of standing in authority over him by allowing him no say in the future of the farm which she and her siblings inherited from their mother. After her father died, when she was in her fifties, she partially fulfilled her childhood dreams by working for a missionary society, although she never went abroad.

4.3   Psychoanalytic perspectives

While feminist theory is useful in identifying why Doreen and Jane became caring daughters, psychoanalytic theory can help us to understand the frustrations and difficulties daughters experienced in being tied to their parents and the conflicts and tensions felt by childless unmarried women caring for children.

splitting
projection The concepts **splitting** and **projection** which relate to our earliest experiences of being mothered are particularly useful here. The term splitting was used by the pioneering psychoanalyst Melanie Klein to show how a baby's helplessness, frustration and dependency on a seemingly omnipotent mother or mother figure are resolved by dividing her into two internal objects: the baby experiences both 'good' and 'bad' feelings towards its mother but disassociates the two sets of feelings from one another. This idea is also helpful in understanding relationships in adult life, particularly those which evoke feelings of dependency or provoke anxiety and contradictory or ambivalent feelings.

In an adult context splitting means marking off and repressing aspects of oneself that are felt to be shameful, unbearable or in some other way intolerable. It acts as a defence to protect one's identity as a particular kind of person. Importantly, for Klein and her followers, splitting (like other defence mechanisms) arises in the context of intimate relationships and is used unconsciously to deal with conflict. Both splitting and projection are *internal* mechanisms used to deal with *external* situations that are experienced as ambiguous and/or threatening. Thus negative feelings towards a loved one, feelings of hatred, envy, anger, aggression, are split off and *projected* into someone else. An important elaboration of the idea of splitting and an

projective identification

extension of the idea of projection is the notion of **projective identification**. This is more than a perception that another person has characteristics too intolerable to recognize in oneself. Rather, it is an unconscious, yet active, process of getting rid of something that resides in the self by putting it 'into' the other. The process of splitting between negative and positive feelings is

idealization

linked to **idealization** and denial on the one hand and demonization and denigration on the other (Gunaratnam and Lewis, 2001).

For an example of this process, we will return once again to the correspondence of the midwife Miss E (discussed in section 3.1) who idealized her own work with mothers and babies in the East End of London and her role as an adopted mother. Evidence that she may have been more ambivalent towards the role of mother than she suggests is shown in another letter where she describes 'the pain of perceiving that the young mother looks upon her child as an unwanted ugly little human animal' (Marie Stopes Papers, 1920, KE to MCS, PP/MCS/A78). While the poor living conditions and frequent unplanned births suffered by many working-class mothers could offer evidence to justify this statement, it is also arguable that Miss E may have been splitting off and denying her own negative feelings about motherhood and expelling or projecting them into working-class mothers.

The continuing close emotional attachment of unmarried daughters towards parents who depended upon them in adult life also seems to have encouraged splitting. Evidence from my own and other researchers' (for example, Lewis and Meredith, 1988) interviews suggests that siblings were especially likely to become the recipients of carers' resentful, angry feelings. Such was the case with Jane, who idealized her mother and split off her own feelings of anger and frustration and projected them into her brother. Since caring was defined as 'women's work' Jane's parents had not expected to receive help from their son and he had done nothing when he came home. When she complained, he had suggested putting their mother in a home. This had deeply shocked Jane, who could only recognize her love for her mother and would not have been able to admit to any similar desires in herself to get rid of her caring responsibilities.

4.4   Unmarried women and paid child care

Feminist and psychoanalytic theories are also useful in analysing tensions and ambivalences experienced by unmarried women employed as primary carers for children in the home. More than 250,000 women worked as live-in or daily nannies before the Second World War (Gathorne-Hardy, 1993), most of whom were either untrained or trained on the job and whose employment conditions were often short-term and insecure. Although few married women engaged in paid work at this time, those who could afford it frequently gave up much, if not all, of the physical care of their children to other (usually unmarried) women, in the same way that they handed over their housework to servants, a strategy that was perceived as important in preserving a family's middle-class status.

The nature of this relationship is worth examining in more detail because it illustrates how care unsettles the boundaries of paid and unpaid work. The feminist philosopher Carol Pateman (1988) has argued that in the unwritten terms of the marriage contract wives have been defined as economic dependants, expected to provide domestic labour, including child care, for their husbands. When middle- and upper-class wives subcontracted services that were supposed to be supplied for love rather than money to working- and lower-middle-class unmarried women, we can see similarities in the terms of that contract with the contract wives had with their husbands. Carers' low wages, paid mainly as board and keep, parallel the housekeeping allowance husbands gave their wives. Equally the freedom from responsibility for the day-to-day care of children that middle-class wives could gain by this means can also be compared to that of a husband – a freedom few working-class wives could expect. It is important therefore to see tensions in mothering created by unmarried women's employment in this area as related not simply to marital status but also to class.

Is this still the case today? Do you think the nature of the contract between mother and carer changes if the mother works outside the home?

However, the analogy between the marriage and carer contracts must not be pushed too far. Although the former was, in theory at least, for life, the contracts between mothers and carers had no such permanence. There were also difficulties for all parties in reconciling a relationship based upon financial gain and the workings of the labour market with its situation in the private sphere and the emotional economy of the family – difficulties many working mothers and carers still experience today. But, while the anxieties and conflicts mothers may have felt through these arrangements could be aired and displaced by referral to the 'servant problem', the interests and needs of the children and the women employed in these capacities were rarely articulated. Relationships had to be negotiated in which much affection might be invested on each side, but their beginnings and endings often depended on the financial position of employers or employees or on other external circumstances such as the children reaching school age.

ACTIVITY 2.6

Read Extract 2.5, from an article ('Four in family') in the magazine *Good Housekeeping*; it describes the life of an unmarried nursery governess through the eyes of her employer. Analyse the power relations.

- Whose point of view is privileged, whose is subordinated and whose is missing?

Extract 2.5   Family life and the governess

[When she] ... thinks of all the intimate clutter that constituted Miss Jenkins's private life now neatly arranged in another chilly bedroom in someone else's house, she must be forgiven if she rails a little over the cruelty of life. Six years of whole-hearted service: six years of as passionate devotion as Miss Jenkins's mild frame can house: six years of a woman's life, and then one day the children look bigger than usual, school bills are heavier than they used to be, and reluctant parents decide they must part with her. So off she goes with her neat trunk to begin all over again.

(*Good Housekeeping*, June 1933, p.10)

COMMENT

This article was written from the perspective of a mother who had contracted the care of her children first to a nanny and subsequently to a nursery governess who both taught and looked after them. On one level, sympathy is being expressed for Miss Jenkins. The terms 'intimate', 'private' and 'passionate devotion' show that she has feelings and a life outside the family. However, the descriptors 'neat' and 'mild' undercut this by suggesting she is incapable of any strong emotions, and her positioning 'in another chilly bedroom in someone else's house' underlines her status as an outsider who can be mocked and pitied. We are invited to sympathize with the parents' economic position which is seen to be the cause of her departure, but while the children are described as having grown to an age when they no longer need her services, no consideration is given to their feelings about her departure. This story contradicts the more comforting stereotype of the nanny who was kept on as a faithful retainer for the rest of her life, a reality in only a minority of wealthier homes.

Memories of lived experience are more complex, as my next example, which privileges the child's perspective, illustrates. The photograph in Figure 2.7 shows my grandfather's upper-middle-class family in the late 1930s.

Figure 2.7   Photograph of the Holden family, c.1936

The woman with a hat is the old nurse who had cared for my grandfather (seated centre) as a baby and who had been retained by the family. Sitting next to her is the governess, Miss Caryer, who took charge of the children when their parents were abroad for long periods in Egypt. Miss Caryer's position in the family was less secure than that of the nurse, yet she was a figure of great importance for one of the children, Ursula (not in the picture), who had recurring nightmares about her parents' departing taxis. In an unpublished autobiographical essay, Ursula remembered her governess with gratitude as having created an 'Eden', giving her 'a security beyond price'.

However, because of Miss Caryer's uneasy status within the household as both paid employee and primary carer, the family could not easily acknowledge the pain her parting might cause. When Ursula was twelve Miss Caryer's taxi eventually came and she hid to avoid seeing her governess's 'distressed red face through the window of the taxi that took her away to her next post' (Holden, undated *c*.1996). Ursula as an adult recognized Miss Caryer's limitations and the constraints of her existence as well as the security she offered. However, her happiest childhood memories are focused very strongly on her governess who is idealized in a way her mother, whom she loved but did not feel at ease with, is not.

Can you see any links to Klein's theory of splitting? Are you able to think of cases in child care where the split is reversed and the mother is idealized and/or the nanny or governess demonized?

We finally reach the carer's viewpoint by examining another oral history interview. Emily (born 1904, interviewed in 1994) said she had not wanted to have children because her own mother had suffered a serious mental illness believed to be hereditary. As a child, Emily had often taken responsibility for her suicidal mother who was admitted permanently to a mental hospital when Emily was 14, and since then had worked as a nanny for a succession of families from the 1920s to the 1960s. She had resolved tensions between the roles of mother and nanny by denying that there was any resemblance between the two and strongly objected to the term 'substitute' mother because it diminished her status:

E   I don't like that word. I just thought it was lovely to be a nanny ... I always thought that to be a nanny would be wonderful and when you're first called nanny it's so wonderful.

KH   Did you feel that your relationship with your children was different from a mother–daughter relationship? Was it different?

E   Oh the children looked on their parents, not later, mostly in the first place, as somebody, a lady who was beautifully dressed and came in, they saw this beautiful lady coming in, they loved her coming in, but there was no rushing up 'mummy, mummy' and tears and arms round their necks, not like nanny. They just knew that they belonged to them, but there was nothing between them. If they were ill or anything else, they might come and say goodnight to them but not always ... cos you see they've got you night and day whatever happens.

For Emily the claims of a birth mother could never rival those of a nanny. While the children may have 'belonged' in a material and legal sense to their mother, emotionally she believed they were hers. When interviewed earlier for a BBC programme she described the 'torture' she experienced when her children's mothers criticized her, and the 'torture' she believed the children felt when they were with their mothers because they 'were quite strangers' to them (Humphries and Gordon, 1993, pp.175–6). Viewed through a psychoanalytic lens, this veiled hostility towards her charges' mothers could be interpreted through the concepts of splitting and projective identification. For Emily the term 'nanny' embodied all the care and nurture which were absent in her own experience of being mothered. She was able to maintain an image of herself as an idealized loving, nurturing figure by splitting off her feelings of anger and frustration about taking on the tasks of motherhood without having the status of a mother and projecting those feelings into mothers who were not there for their children in the way that a nanny was.

The contract she held with her children's mothers left her in a subordinate position. Mothers wielded financial power and were the ultimate authority in their children's lives, so Emily's subservient status made it difficult for her to be openly critical of her employers. The reality was that she could not always be there for the children and had faced the pain of frequent partings:

KH *How did you feel about leaving the children?*

E   I was ill. I had to go back and see them. I really was ill. But then I saw that they were alright. I said I wouldn't get fond of children again ...

KH *Did it occur to you to stay on?*

E   No. They were having the governess by then and the little one was going to be with the governess so there was really nothing more for me to do.

Emily had managed to stay in touch with most of her charges and had put them all together into one photo frame, a strange family whose changing fashions showed them to span the forty years of her working life. There is poignancy in her attempt to gather together children who had never known one another and whose relationship to her relied on their continuing loyalty to a nanny who had been compelled to leave them when they were still quite young; for ultimately, they were not her children.

5   Conclusion

Returning to the point made in the introduction that this chapter would cast new light on the way in which care is constructed today, there are a number of key issues to be reinforced here. First, since the Second World War, the decline in the proportion of older unmarried women in the population has been accompanied by changed expectations in relation to work and sexuality. Unmarried women are no longer expected to sublimate their sexual energy into caring for other people's children, nor are they as willing to dedicate their professional or personal lives in service to other families. Yet the difficulty many of us have in making clear boundaries between paid and unpaid caring work is still a live issue. The limited character of social policies to support working parents has intensified the deep anxieties many parents feel about paying another person to care for their children. The installation of 'nanny watch' cameras, the demonization of the British nanny Louise Woodward by the media in both the USA and Britain in 1997 and the exposure of selfish, cruel parents who exploit carers by two American nannies in the best-selling novel, *The Nanny Diaries* (Krause and McLaughlin, 2002), suggest that parents and nannies still often idealize their own relationships with children by splitting off their negative feelings and projecting them into others.

Second, the fact that unmarried women are now less likely to live with their parents and more likely to place a higher value on their careers and on individual fulfilment than in the past has important implications. Unmarried women's caring responsibilities were finally recognized in 1965 when the Rev. Mary Webster set up the National Council for the Single Woman and her Dependants, but its change of name in the 1980s to the National Council of Carers reflected the reduction in the number of single women willing or able to give care. With an increasingly ageing population, this left a gap which the state has been reluctant to fill, increasing the pressure on working families still further. While still often ridiculed, the disappearance of the unmarried woman carer has also been mourned. Yet it is still more often women, married and unmarried, who take on the main responsibility of parental support.

Finally, by drawing upon feminist and psychoanalytic theory to analyse interview and autobiographical data, we have been able to gain a closer understanding of the internal dynamics of unmarried women's caring relationships. These methodological approaches have been shown to be useful in uncovering conflicts, tensions and ambivalent feelings, bringing out both the pleasures women gained from becoming carers and the personal costs involved in caring. Most importantly, both the theory and the sources used in this chapter as a whole have allowed us to see that social policies which reinforced gendered norms in relation to care were not rigidly deterministic. While such policies and norms were influential in shaping caring identities, women also consciously and unconsciously drew upon these identities to further their own individual interests and aspirations in their 'public' and 'private' lives.

Further resources

If you want to explore some of the issues relating to marriage, class and employment raised in this chapter, you could look at Jane Lewis's *Women in England 1870–1950* (1984) which provides a broad historical overview. In a related way, Diana Gittens's 'Marital status, work and kinship, 1850–1930' (1986) illustrates the family responsibilities of married and single daughters, while the relationships between servants and mistresses are considered in Judy Giles's *Women, Identity and Private Life in Britain, 1900–1950* (1995). Katherine Holden's discussion of the spinster's relationship to the family in 'Family shadows: unmarried women' (1999) demonstrates how unmarried women's identities in the inter-war years were forged through their familial roles, but also how intimate relationships between unrelated adults and children were constructed. A more detailed consideration of unmarried women's involvement in unpaid care work can be found in her chapter 'Family care and unpaid work' (2001). The novel *The Nanny Diaries* (Krause and McLaughlin, 2002) – based on the experiences of two nannies working in the USA – illustrates the tensions in the relationship between nannies and mothers and the value of the notion of 'splitting' for analysing those dynamics.

An extremely comprehensive bibliography of historical and contemporary sources on single women (including single mothers) can be found at: http://www.medusanet.ca/singlewomen/resource.htm (accessed on 14 November 2003).

References

Beddoe, D. (1989) *Back to Home and Duty: Women Between the Wars, 1918– 1939*, London, Pandora.

Carabine, J. (2004a) 'Sexualities, personal lives and social policy' in Carabine (2004b).

Carabine, J. (ed.) (2004b) *Sexualities: Personal Lives and Social Policy*, Bristol, The Policy Press in association with The Open University.

Chandler, J. (1991) *Women Without Husbands: An Exploration of the Margins of Marriage*, London, Macmillan.

Dalley, G. (1988) *Ideologies of Caring: Rethinking Community and Collectivism*, London, Macmillan.

Doolittle, M. (2004) 'Sexuality, parenthood and population: explaining fertility decline in Britain from the 1860s to 1920s' in Carabine (2004b).

Douglas, M. (1991) *Purity and Danger: An Analysis of the Concepts of Pollution and Taboo* (3rd edn), London, Routledge.

Finch, J. (1989) *Family Obligations and Social Change*, Cambridge, Polity Press.

Gathorne-Hardy, J. (1993) *The Rise and Fall of the British Nanny*, London, Weidenfeld and Nicolson.

Giles, J. (1995) *Women, Identity and Private Life in Britain, 1900–1950*, London, Macmillan.

Gilligan, C. (1982) *In a Different Voice. Psychological Theory and Women's Development*, Cambridge, MA, Harvard University Press.

Gittens, D. (1986) 'Marital status, work and kinship 1850–1930' in Lewis, J. (ed.) *Labour of Love: Women's Experiences of Home and Family, 1850–1940*, London, Blackwell.

Gothard, J. (1990) 'The healthy wholesome British domestic girl: single female migration and the Empire Settlement Act, 1922–1930', in Constantine, S. (ed.)

Emigrants and Empire, British Settlement in the Dominions Between the Wars, Manchester, Manchester University Press.

Graham, E. (1965) *The Children who Lived in a Barn*, Harmondsworth, Penguin (Puffin edition).

Graham, H. (1983) 'Caring: a labour of love' in Finch, J. and Groves, D. (eds) *A Labour of Love: Women, Work and Caring*, London, Routledge and Kegan Paul.

Gunaratnam, Y. and Lewis, G. (2001) 'Racializing emotional labour and emotionalizing racialized labour: anger, fear and shame in social welfare', *Journal of Social Work Practice*, vol.15, no.2, pp.131–48.

Hall, S. (1997) 'The spectacle of the "other"' in Hall, S. (ed.) *Representation: Cultural Representations and Signifying Practices,* London, Sage in association with The Open University.

Heath-Stubbs, M. (1935) *Friendships Highway: Being the History of the Girls' Friendly Society, 1875–1935*, London, GFS Central Office.

Holden, K. (1996) 'The shadow of marriage: single women in England, 1919–1939', unpublished PhD thesis, University of Essex.

Holden, K. (1999) 'Family shadows: unmarried women' in Davidoff, L., Doolittle, M., Fink, J. and Holden, K. *The Family Story: Blood, Contract and Intimacy, 1830–1960*, London, Longman.

Holden, K. (2001) 'Family care and unpaid work' in Zweiniger-Bargielowska, I. (ed.) *Women in Twentieth-Century Britain*, Harlow, Longman.

Holden, U. (undated, *c.*1996) 'Miss Caryer', unpublished.

Humphries, S. and Gordon, P. (1993) *Labour of Love, The Experience of Parenthood in Britain 1900–1950*, London, Sedgwick and Jackson.

Jeffreys, M. (1985) *The Spinster and Her Enemies: Feminism and Sexuality*, London, Pandora.

Krause, N. and McLaughlin, E. (2002) *The Nanny Diaries*, Harmondsworth, Penguin.

Lennon, M., McAdam, M. and O'Brien, J. (1988) *Across the Water: Irish Women's Lives in Britain*, London, Virago.

Lewis, J. (1984) *Women in England, 1870–1950*, Hemel Hempstead, Harvester Wheatsheaf.

Lewis, J. and Meredith, B. (1988) *Daughters Who Care: Daughters Caring for Mothers at Home*, London, Routledge.

Marie Stopes Papers (1920/1921) *Archives and Manuscripts*, London, The Wellcome Library for the History and Understanding of Medicine.

Nolan, J. (1989) *Ourselves Alone: Women's Emigration from Ireland 1885–1920*, Kentucky, KY, The University Press of Kentucky.

Oram, A. (1989) 'Embittered, sexless or homosexual: attacks on spinster teachers 1918–1939' in Lesbian History Group (eds) *Not a Passing Phase: Recovering Lesbians in History 1840–1985*, London, Women's Press.

Oram, A. (1992) 'Repressed and thwarted, or bearer of the New World? The spinster in interwar feminist discourses', *Women's History Review*, vol.1, no.3, pp.413–34.

Pateman, C. (1988) *The Sexual Contract*, Cambridge, Polity Press.

Stopes, M. (1918) *Married Love: A New Contribution to the Solution of Sex Difficulties*, London, G.P. Putnam and Sons.

Stopes, M. (1920) *Radiant Motherhood*, London, G.P. Putnam and Sons.

Taylor, P. (1979) 'Daughters and mistresses – mothers and maids: domestic service between the wars' in Clarke, J., Critcher, C. and Johnson, R. (eds) *Working Class Culture, Studies in History and Theory*, London, Hutchinson.

Walter, B. (2001) *Outsiders Inside: Whiteness, Place and Irish Women*, London, Routledge.

Ware, V. (1992) *Beyond the Pale: White Women, Racism and History*, London, Verso.

Waters, C. (2000) 'Autobiography, nostalgia and the changing practices of working-class selfhood' in Belmer, G.K. and Leventhal, F.M. (eds) (2000) *Tradition, Nostalgia and Identity in Modern British Culture*, Stanford, CA, Stanford University Press.

Widdowson, E. (2004) 'Retiring lives? Old age, work and welfare' in Mooney, G. (ed.) *Work: Personal Lives and Social Policy*, Bristol, The Policy Press in association with The Open University.

Willmott, P. (1992) *A Singular Woman: The Life of Geraldine Aves 1898–1986*, London, Whiting and Birch.

CHAPTER 3

Victims or Threats? Children, Care and Control

by Barry Goldson

Contents

1 Introduction

The fact that we all experience childhood is one of the most unifying features of the human condition – we all 'know' what it is to be a child. Moreover, in the UK we claim to believe that childhood should comprise a protected stage of life, insulated from the troubles of the adult world. As Chris Jenks (1996, p.8) has observed, 'childhood is taken for granted, it is regarded as necessary and inevitable, and thus part of normal life – its utter "thereness" seems to foster a complacent attitude'. Such 'complacency' is, in many respects, further bolstered by the provisions of domestic law – together with international conventions, standards, treaties and rules – which state that children must be cared for and looked after, both in the private domain of the family and in the public sphere of health, welfare, education and leisure services. It follows that social policies should provide children with opportunities to enjoy healthy and happy personal lives, and the same policies should aim to respect and uphold children's rights (Saraga, 1998).

In 1990 the World Summit on Children assembled in New York, constituting the largest gathering of state leaders in history. They declared that the 'well-being of children requires political action at the highest level', and they pledged: 'we are determined to take that action. We ourselves make a solemn commitment to give high priority to the rights of children' (quoted in Children's Rights Development Unit, 1994, p.xi). The United Nations Convention on the Rights of the Child (UNCRC) was seen to embody such commitment and it was soon formally adopted by 169 countries. The UNCRC set out the principles and detailed standards for the rights of children, the care of children, laws, policies and practices which impact on children, and for both formal and informal relationships with children. With some exceptions – perhaps most notably the USA – the UNCRC was accepted more quickly and more comprehensively than any other international convention and the UK government ratified it in 1991.

It is important to acknowledge such advances in formal international standards, national legislation and the social policies that might flow from them. However, it is also imperative to measure progress not simply in terms of conventional obligations and the provisions of statute and policy, but against the lived experiences and personal lives of children themselves. In this sense children are both human beings and human 'becomings'. The developmental trajectory of their personal lives may not be absolutely determined by their particular social circumstances and the specificities of institutional interventions, but such material contexts will make a substantial claim in shaping 'the personal'. It is largely for this reason that it is necessary to look beyond the 'world at the level of appearances' (Wright, 1979) and to disturb the accepting, commonsensical 'complacency' to which we referred above. This means questioning oversimplified and benign conceptualizations of care as addressing the needs and rights of the child, and considering the extent to which the same laws, policies and practices permit the exercise of adult or state power in ways that subject children to formal control. In other words, in thinking about what is done *for* children, we also need to consider what is done *to* them.

This distinction between 'doing for' (caring) and 'doing to' (controlling) children, is particularly important when we consider the personal lives of children who endure disadvantaged childhoods. For the purposes here, this is taken to mean childhoods that are framed within adverse material conditions where the combined effects of poverty, inequalities and social injustices can have a corrosive effect on children; their families (however they are formed); their housing conditions; their educational opportunities; their leisure activities; and their general health and well-being (Goldson et al., 2002). Inevitably perhaps, this is where the caring and controlling sites of policy-makers and state agencies are often most sharply focused, and this chapter considers the means by which the above conditions are produced and reproduced, the impact that disadvantage can have on the personal lives of children, and the role of social policy and institutional arrangements in creating and/or obviating such phenomena. More specifically still, our discussion and analysis concentrates upon the personal lives of children who are cared for, and/or controlled, within institutions – specific spaces and places of care and control – and the social policies that frame institutional interventions and practices.

Examining care and control in this way is helpful, in as much as it identifies some of the problems that are often associated with convenient – but oversimplified – conceptualizations, and it begins to introduce inevitable complexities. It also serves to question the 'official' rationale that underpins convention and statute, and signals the possible dissonance between the provisions and prescriptions of law, policy and practice on the one hand, and the impact on children's personal lives on the other. However, while this is an important exercise in policy analysis, such probing and questioning can sometimes seem confusing. Further unpacking and clarification is necessary therefore, and in section 2 and throughout the chapter as a whole, we consider a range of crucial and related questions. Is there a unifying concept of childhood? How is childhood shaped and socially constructed? Why do we conceive of certain constituencies of children as victims in need of special care and protection, and others as threats requiring control and even punishment? What institutional arrangements have been put in place to administer care and control for different groups of children? Can care and control be so readily compartmentalized? Is care possible without an element of control, and can control itself be caring? Such questions are especially important in view of the fact that the social circumstances, material contexts and, more often than not, the behaviours and needs of children who are differentiated and classified in this way, are in reality remarkably similar.

Aims By addressing the above questions, and applying them to a more detailed critical analysis, this chapter has five primary aims:

- To problematize and interrogate the concept of 'child care'.

- To focus upon the personal lives of disadvantaged children, and to critically examine the driving imperatives that shape social policy responses to such children within historical and contemporary contexts (primarily in England and Wales).

care
victims
control
threats

- To explore the development of institutions that are designed to '**care**' for children perceived as '**victims**', and to '**control**' those regarded as '**threats**'.

- To critically assess the policies which underpin these institutions, and to question the legitimacy of the institutions themselves.

- To illustrate some of the difficult tensions within such institutions by drawing upon primary research and by giving 'voice' to children and staff alike.

These aims are not ranked or addressed in any order of importance, rather they are integrated within and across the chapter.

2   Key concepts

Given that we have already introduced certain complexities into our discussion and analysis, it is worthwhile paying further attention to some of the key concepts that underpin this chapter. This section considers: the means by which childhood is socially constructed; the way in which children can be perceived either as 'victims' or as 'threats'; and the range of responses that such perceptions can activate in terms of caring or controlling interventions.

2.1   Social constructions of childhood

childhood

In modern society, the roles ascribed to children and the meanings attributed to the term **childhood** are different to those that prevailed at earlier moments in our history. These roles and meanings will also vary across the countries of the world, and the personal lives of children will be shaped in accordance with particular cultural norms and conventions. Furthermore, within any discrete place, and at any specific moment, children will not necessarily experience childhood in the same way. The nature of their personal lives will differ, and the contours and co-ordinates that frame their everyday experiences will be affected by structural conditions including the social divisions of class, 'race', gender, sexuality and disability. In other words, concepts and definitions of childhood vary widely across the boundaries of time, place and social position. By applying this type of analysis we can see that the meanings of childhood and the experiences of being a child are **socially constructed** (Saraga, 1998).

socially constructed

The social constructionist paradigm poses a fundamental challenge to biological and/or universalistic notions that suggest that childhood is little more than a 'naturally' defined, age-determined life stage, which remains essentially constant irrespective of the specificities of historical moment and/or geographical place. Such a challenge does not deny the significance of human biology, but rather it shifts the focus from biological determinism to the conceptual relativity of childhood within history. In other words childhood is not regarded as a naturally fixed and static state of being, but rather a 'moving image' which changes through time and across space. In this sense the definition of terms such as 'child', 'children' and 'childhood' are relative, uncertain and changing, as distinct from absolute, fixed and static. We will return to the means by which childhood has been shaped through history in more detail in section 3.

In examining constructions of childhood, social constructionist analysis assesses the extent to which childhood is, or should be, differentiated from 'adulthood' – it explores the origin, purpose and consequence of such **inter-generational differentiation**. Put simply, the primary questions are: what are the relations between childhood and adulthood, and how and why is childhood and the personal lives of children different to adulthood and the personal lives of adults? This is important because it affords childhood its own conceptual space and it provides for a sociological analysis of childhood in and of itself, as distinct from simply comparing and contrasting childhood with adulthood. Thus, childhood is seen as important for what it is in addition to what it becomes, and children are conceptualized as human beings as well as 'human becomings'.

er-generational differentiation

ra-generational distinction

Equally significant to inter-generational analysis is the question of **intra-generational distinction** because this helps us to understand that at any given time and place children's experiences of childhood will be shaped by their specific social–structural locations. The primary emphasis is not with the individual child however – although this has a value of its own – but with the distinctive structural conditions within which childhood is lived and experienced: the relations of class, 'race', gender, sexuality and disability, to which we referred above. The key questions here engage with the plurality of childhood and the notion of **childhoods**, and they demand the deconstruction of oversimplified monolithic concepts. Thus there is a range of childhoods: working class, middle class, black, white, male, female, gay/lesbian, heterosexual, 'able bodied' and 'disabled'; and childhood is additionally differentiated across the complex intersections within and between these broad structural relations. Furthermore, in a divided and unequal society (such as the UK) in which profound injustices are lodged within class-based antagonisms, institutionalized racism, patriarchal relations, homophobia and disablism, it follows that some children are privileged while others are disadvantaged. Tony Novak has illustrated this point by contrasting the fortunes of rich children and poor children, and two quotations from his work provide examples of the ways in which class and 'race' can impact upon childhood:

childhoods

> The cementing of class inequalities begins at an early age, and among the myriad of ways in which the privileges, or deprivations, of social class are passed down from one generation to the next, formal educational systems figure centrally. Schooling both reflects childhood inequalities and reinforces them.
>
> (Novak, 2002, p.65)

> All [minoritized] children are more likely to experience poverty than white children but for black and Pakistani and Bangladeshi children the risk is much,

much higher: 74 per cent of Pakistani and Bangladeshi children live in
households with incomes less than half the national average, as do 57 per cent of
black children, compared with 34 per cent of children as a whole.

(Novak, 2002, p.62)

Novak identifies the education system as a primary site upon which class-
based privileges and disadvantages are produced and reproduced, and he also
exposes the consequences of institutionalized racism in respect of the
'racialization' of child poverty.

Children's opportunities are also differentiated along social–structural lines in
many other ways. Indeed it would be possible, although in a chapter such as
this not practical, to detail the whole spectrum of inequalities and injustices
which impact upon the personal lives of children. Privileges are reserved for
the few, while many others endure disadvantaged childhoods, however they
are nuanced. It is normally within the most disadvantaged childhood
constituencies that some children are perceived to be victims while others are
regarded as threats, and it is at the level of intra-generational analysis
therefore, that questions of care and control are particularly salient.

2.2   Victims or threats?

The social constructionist perspective questions the idealized image of
childhood as a period of innocence, boundless joy and protection from the
harshness of the adult world. Many children's personal lives are scarred by
injustice and inequality and are not necessarily located comfortably within
contexts of care. We might expect this to trigger compensatory responses from
social policy, with special attention universally afforded to disadvantaged
children in order to redress care and welfare deficits. However, the situation is
more complex than this, and such complexity is largely derived from a
dualistic conception of childhood itself (Hendrick, 1994).

This dualistic conception means that particular constituencies of children are
commonly perceived either as vulnerable victims in need of care and
protection, or as precocious threats who require control and correction. As we
have noted, this way of seeing tends to focus – particularly through class-
based, racialized and gendered lenses – upon children who are most exposed
to structural disadvantage. Furthermore, such dualism not only raises issues
about the protection of the child, but it also introduces the question of
protection *from* the child. It follows that state policy responses and the
practical interventions of state agencies have been driven both by the
imperatives of care, welfare and protection (in relation to child 'victims'), and
the priorities of control, regulation and punishment (in respect of child
'threats'). Although such binary classification is oversimplified, it nevertheless
further emphasizes the inadequacy of totalizing definitions of children and
childhood, and it challenges any unifying concept of care itself. In
contemporary times victim–threat dualism is particularly marked, and the
special 'vulnerabilities' of some children (such as those at risk of abuse and
violation from adults – usually men), and the 'anti-social behaviour' of a

different constituency of children (including child 'offenders'), dominates popular discourse, political reaction and policy response (Scraton, 1997).

Take a look at the two newspaper headlines in Figure 3.1 and consider the language that is being used to represent the children involved.

Figure 3.1   Newspaper headlines

The first headline reports the findings of a public inquiry into the tragic death of 8-year-old Victoria Climbié, a victim of violence, and ultimately murder, at the hands of her adult guardians. The headline clearly represents this child as a 'victim', whose manifest needs for care and protection were denied by abusive guardians and overlooked by 'failing' child protection services including those of police, health and social service agencies. The second headline represents a different construction of children however. Here the focus is on the perceived 'threat' that child 'thugs' and 'yobs' might pose. The emphasis shifts from a construction of the vulnerable 'victim child' in need of protection, to a representation of the menacing 'threatening child' requiring control and correction. The intrinsic compassion of the first headline is substituted by the dismissive impatience of the second.

Such contrasting victim–threat constructions of children are not confined to newspaper coverage and popular discourse; they are also institutionalized through official policy documents as shown in Figure 3.2.

The first policy document, *Safeguarding Children*, was prepared by the Chief Inspectors of many key state services. It sets out the care needs of child 'victims' and examines the arrangements for meeting such needs. The second document, *No More Excuses*, is a government White Paper, which is a serious statement of policy that lays down a range of controlling responses with regard to child 'threats'. In many respects the newspaper extracts and the policy documents can be seen to mirror each other, and in each, a specific construction of children and childhood is expressed.

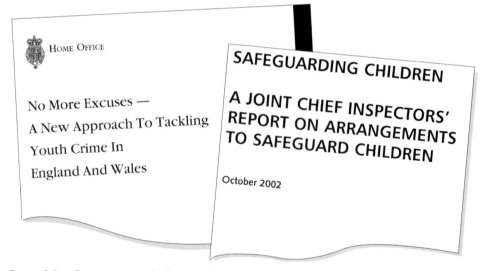

Figure 3.2   Front covers of official policy documents

ACTIVITY 3.2

Reflect on the points that have been made so far about the different constructions of childhood and jot down your responses to the following: what are the likely consequences of victim–threat dualism for children: for the way in which they are perceived; for the responses that they attract from official agencies; for the services that they receive; and for the specific nature of formal interventions?

COMMENT

In section 3 we chart the historical origins of victim–threat dualism, and its most contemporary manifestations are examined in section 4. For now however, it is important to re-emphasize that such contrasting conceptualizations are almost exclusively reserved for children who grow up in the most disadvantaged social–structural circumstances. In this way, and in many important respects, the personal circumstances and backgrounds of children perceived to be victims and those regarded as threats are strikingly similar. However, the victim–threat dichotomy tends to underpin contrasting notions of deservingness and it informs the deserving–undeserving construction, which has also been present throughout history (albeit in variable forms at different moments in time) and remains today as shown in the newspaper extracts and policy documents in Figures 3.1 and 3.2. This means that particular services are largely reserved for children who are thought to be 'deserving', while quite different (and usually less favourable) responses are targeted at their 'undeserving' counterparts.

2.3 Care and control

We have already established that the concepts of care and control do not lend themselves to easy definition. This reinforces the observations in Chapter 1 that the ideas and meanings afforded to care are problematic and efforts to define and regulate the meanings and practices of care are the subject of intense contestation and contradiction. Indeed when 'control' is factored into the equation, such 'contestation and contradiction' becomes even more complex.

Stanley Cohen (1985, p.1) defines social control as 'the organized ways in which society responds to behaviour and people it regards as deviant, problematic, worrying, threatening, troublesome or undesirable in some way or another'. On one level this appears to be very straightforward. It implies that control is necessary in order to *protect* the conforming majority and to *contain* the wayward minority. This mode of control is perhaps most recognizable within systems of criminal law and justice. It is commonly underpinned by notions of punishment, deterrence, segregation and social defence, and it is normally derived in reactive emotions including retribution, revenge and retaliation. However, conceptualizations of control can also embrace concepts such as treatment, prevention, rehabilitation and reform, which are in turn informed by more benign emotions such as compassion and benevolence. Thus, the meaning of control is not quite as straightforward as it first seems. In this way, as Cohen (1985, p.2) himself reminds us, control is an extraordinarily broad-based concept which can 'cover all social processes to induce conformity ranging from infant socialization [otherwise known as child care] through to public execution'. Moreover, control is not only expressed through the more overtly coercive apparatus of the state (for example, police, courts and prisons), but also through seemingly more benign services (such as health, education and welfare). Rather than perceiving care and control as diametrical opposites, we can begin to see how the boundaries overlap. In other words control can imply care, just as care can imply control.

ACTIVITY 3.3

By reflecting on your own childhood and considering the notions of care and control that we have discussed thus far, can you remember occasions when boundaries appeared to overlap?

COMMENT

You may recall occasions when parents, relatives, carers, teachers or other adults in authority, acted in ways that appeared to be responsible and caring to them and others, but were experienced by you as unwelcome interference and unjustifiable control. Equally, with the benefit of hindsight, you might recollect instances when what felt like the unnecessary exercise of adult control was actually a genuine expression of care. It is also likely that your experiences operated at both the informal and formal level, within both the 'private' realm of family life and the 'public' realm of state services (for example schools). Indeed, this links to wider arrangements within the UK which provide for the care and control of children. A relation between 'the family' and the state is forged within which caring obligations towards children, and the right to exercise authority and control over them, is negotiated and defined.

The relation between the state and 'the family' – which in this context is usually taken to mean the 'conventional' nuclear family 'headed' by heterosexual married parents – is both consensual (in the sense that the family is the preferred social institution in which to bear and to rear children) and contested (in that the nature and boundaries of the relation are dynamic).

However, not all families are able or considered 'suitable' to raise and socialize children. This particularly applies when a child's health, welfare and well-being is considered to be at risk (the child as victim), and/or where the child's behaviour transgresses normative or legal boundaries (the child as threat). This is the root of family/state contestation whereby children within such families attract the gaze of state agencies and are exposed to state-directed interventions. Such interventions may be conceptualized primarily as caring and protective (as in the child care functions of social services departments), or controlling and corrective (as with the interventions of criminal justice agencies). As we have already seen however, there is almost certainly overlap and intersection in and between each of these functions. At the extremes of such interventions, as Lea Shamgar-Handelman (1994, p.261) observes, 'the state and/or authorized agencies have legal power to deny the right of some families to raise the children who were born to them'. In such cases, children may be re-situated within substitute families (fostered or adopted), or placed within caring or corrective institutions (children's homes or penal facilities). Furthermore, contingent upon the degree of victimization and risk that the child is thought to face, or the extent of the threat that they are adjudged to pose, the institutional setting may be 'open' (unlocked) or 'secure' (locked).

3   The origins of modern institutions

The issues that we have discussed in sections 1 and 2 did not suddenly materialize at the beginning of the twenty-first century. Rather, they have emerged, developed and consolidated over time, with deep-rooted historical antecedents dating back to the early part of the nineteenth century. In mapping the processes of policy development and reform, it is important to appreciate their social context, the economic and political interests behind them, their internal paradoxes and the nature of their appeal in respect of both care and control. Although schematic, and inevitably incomplete, this section critically examines the social and economic conditions within which the personal lives of disadvantaged children were located and constituted, and the context within which specific institutions for their care and control emerged and developed. Our focus is primarily England and Wales.

3.1   Social crises and the institutional 'fix'

Throughout the first half of the nineteenth century – the period of industrial revolution – the scale and nature of change profoundly unsettled the social, economic and political equilibrium. Wholesale internal migration – from the country to the rapidly growing towns and cities – was unprecedented, and the new urban populations were starkly polarized along the lines of poverty and wealth. Philanthropy, social reform and 'child saving' began to emerge around this time and this dovetailed into widespread moral anxieties and political concerns. The philanthropists were moved by their revulsion at the appalling conditions endured by the children of the poor, and the Establishment was concerned with the prospect of major social unrest, if not revolution. Action was legitimized on both counts (Lewis, 1998). The prevailing view was that society needed to protect and care for child victims (especially the increasing numbers of abandoned 'street children'), but it also needed to be protected from the perceived threat that others ('juvenile delinquents') posed, and to control them as necessary. The 'solution' to each problem was to be found in specific institutions.

The social construction of childhood, as a separate and independent life stage from adulthood (what we called 'inter-generational differentiation' in section 2.1), had yet to be fully institutionalized. There was no formal system of child welfare for vulnerable children (victims), and the practices of the criminal justice and penal systems – where child and adult offenders (threats) were treated alike – raised particular concerns (Goldson, 2002b). Margaret May explains:

> For the first time the crucial question of the suitability of imprisonment for children was raised ... underpinned by both emotional and practical considerations. The contrast between a small vulnerable child and the fortress-like condition of the prison affronted the growing humanitarian sentiment at the time. But it was the new awareness among prison officials of children's reactions to confinement which engendered reform ... Crawford and Russell [influential prison inspectors] found that cellular isolation clearly revealed the mental and physical

differences between children and adults, and concluded, 'so marked is the distinction in the feeling and habit of manhood and youth that it is quite impractical to engraft any beneficial plan for the lengthened confinement of boys upon a system adapted to adults'.

(May, 1973/2002, pp.100–1)

You can see from Figure 3.3 that very young children were treated and processed in precisely the same way as adults. This 11-year-old boy was locked-up alongside adult prisoners.

By the mid nineteenth century, philanthropists, social reformers and voluntary organizations were particularly influential in mobilizing support for the creation of new institutions for children *outside* of the formal prison system. Significantly however, these institutions would provide not only for those adjudged to be threats, but also for those perceived to be victims. Such developments were driven by the consolidating social construction of the particular needs of the child on the one hand, and the developing consensus with regard to the role of families on the other. Families were expected to provide care for children, and exercise control over them, and where parents were regarded as being unable or unwilling to fulfil such functions, institutional intervention was increasingly legitimized.

One of the most prominent champions of specialist institutions for children was Mary Carpenter, whose prescriptions for the treatment of both the 'destitute' (*deprived* victims) and the 'delinquent' (*depraved* threats) were recorded in her extensive writings (Carpenter, 1851, 1853). Carpenter and other leading reformers claimed that the unifying characteristic of all 'outcast children' was moral deficit – resulting from parental failure and neglect – and they believed that the prospect of individual reform and moral reclamation was the basis for intervention. The victim–threat dualism, expressed as a
deserving–undeserving distinction, was particularly evident in the insistence by Mary Carpenter and other reformers on separate institutions. Although the social–structural circumstances of the children who filled the institutions were very *similar*, the developing thrust of social policy and institutional practice contrived to categorize them by using a crude binary classification. In this way each 'category' of child was treated quite *differently*. In 1854 the Youthful Offenders Act allowed courts to send children convicted of an offence to a reformatory school for between two and five years (controlling the threats). In 1857 the Industrial Schools Act provided that children who were found begging, suffering from parental neglect and/or seemingly beyond parental control could be sent *indefinitely* to an industrial school (caring for victims).

deserving–
undeserving

On one level the new institutions – which were managed by voluntary associations with state funding, and were subject to state inspection and certification – can be conceptualized in terms of humanitarian reform. On another level however, the reformatories and the industrial schools also extended the reach of state intervention into working-class family life, and ultimately intensified the depth of social control over the most disadvantaged children. By the end of the nineteenth century, more than 30,000 children were contained in one or other form of institution, and recognizably modern constructs of the institutional arrangements for 'caring' for child 'victims' and

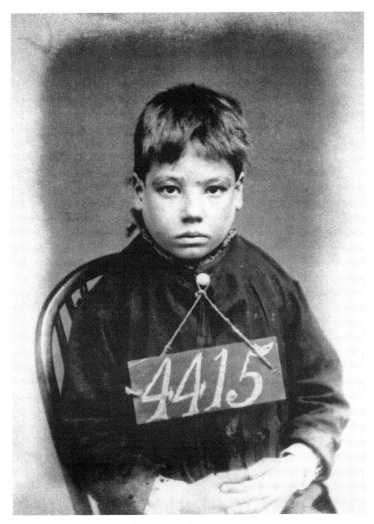

Figure 3.3   James Leadbetter, child prisoner

'controlling' child 'threats' had been established. The reforms had ushered in a new disciplinary network targeted at the poorest children and families, and underpinned by a spurious form of classification.

3.2 Emerging and enduring concerns

With regard to the emergence and consolidation of the institutional 'fix', four key concerns are particularly noteworthy.

First, the policy and practice developments that unfolded throughout the nineteenth century were largely informed by notions of (in)discipline, (im)morality and (ir)responsibility. Within this context, the legitimacy of state intervention in respect of 'malfunctioning' or 'dysfunctional' families was increasingly expressed. It was not simply the principle of state intervention that emerged, but also issues of sanction and punishment as Allison Morris and Henri Giller have explained:

> This marked the start of the state's promotion of desired family life and
> intervention to enforce it. In England, for example, in the 1870s and 1880s,
> various Acts of Parliament required parents to carry out certain parental duties by
> the threat of a penalty or even the loss of the child if they failed.
>
> (Morris and Giller, 1987, p.22)

Indeed, parenting and 'the family' occupied a central position within social
policy discourses in relation to the care and control of children, which
continues to this day. In this way, an essentially moralistic gaze has tended to
focus upon disadvantaged children and families. More specifically, parental
responsibility and children's individual agency are emphasized, while the
significance of structural conditions and material realities (principally poverty,
inequality and injustice) are largely neglected. Personal lives and individual
behaviours are thus abstracted from their material contexts, or to put it
another way: 'the remedy of social problems [is seen to lie] primarily in
personal rejuvenation rather than in the more politically radical solution of
changing fundamental aspects of the social structure' (Morris and Giller, 1987,
p.20). In many respects the institutions that are designed to care for, and
control, children outside of 'the family' have always been expected to 'treat'
the casualties of injustice and inequality without disturbing the status quo.
This is as true for modern institutions as it was for the reformatories and
industrial schools and we consider this contention further in sections 4.1 and
4.2.

Second, the institutionalization of disadvantaged children from the nineteenth
century onwards has not only been class specific, but it is largely racialized
and gendered too. (We consider the question of 'race' in more detail in section
4.2.) In reflecting upon gendered practices in the mid nineteenth century for
example, Heather Shore (2002, p.166) has noted that 'boys and girls were
treated differently, and that the differences extended to the likelihood of
spending time within the formal mechanisms of the criminal justice system'.
Although it was not unknown for girls to be contained within prisons (and
later in reformatory schools), their offending was largely confined to petty
thefts and other low-level acquisitive offences. Only rarely were girls
convicted of more serious charges and offences against the person. Indeed,
girls were far more likely to be perceived as 'victims', and accordingly held in
the more 'care' oriented industrial schools on the basis of 'sexual delinquency'
and 'sexual immorality'. This is not to say that leniency prevailed. As we noted
in section 3.1, fixed-term sentences did not apply to industrial schools and the
institutional processes addressing the 'care' of girls therefore, were more
open-ended and less determinate than those which related to the 'control' of
boys. Shore observes:

> girls entering the industrial school had often been criminalized as a result of
> association with sexual immorality. In contrast ... such circumstances were hardly
> significant in boys' cases ... the unavoidable conclusion is that it was the control of
> female sexuality that was the key aim.
>
> (Shore, 2002, p.168)

This pattern of gendered institutionalization continues to apply to this day (Goldson, 2002c; O'Neill, 2001) and we return to this point in section 4.2.

Third, although our focus is primarily on England and Wales, the structural conditions that framed children's personal lives, the discourses of care and control, and the ideological imperatives that underpinned the social policies and institutional arrangements which were established in order to respond to them in the nineteenth century, also applied elsewhere. Shore notes (2002, p.167) that in the nineteenth century 'contemporaries were turning to foreign models for inspiration ... [institutions] in Rauhe Haus in Germany and Mettray in France were visited by the luminaries of the British juvenile justice system'. In more recent times many countries have managed to move beyond and/or severely limit their use of institutions for the care and control of children. In England and Wales however, a peculiar attachment to the institutional 'fix' has prevailed, and the relatively widespread reliance on institutional responses and separate systems for the care and control of child victims and threats has endured. Indeed, at the beginning of the twenty-first century proportionately more children are locked-up in England and Wales than in almost any other country in the European Union (Goldson, 2002a, 2002c).

Fourth, there is a disjuncture between the rhetorical claims that were made on behalf of the institutions for the care and control of children, and the day-to-day operational realities and regime practices that framed the personal lives of children within them. The institutions were austere places as we can see from the picture of the Mettray reformatory school in France, which was widely commended and ultimately emulated by the British reformers.

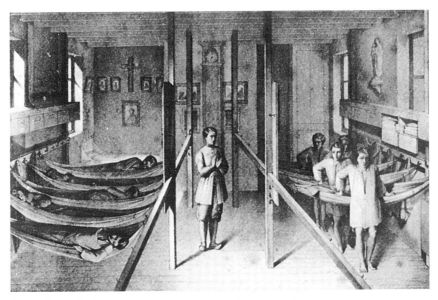

Figure 3.4   Bedtime at the reformatory at Mettray in France

In addition to the physical environment of the institutions, the routines, regimes and operational practices were also problematic. The rhetorical emphasis on treatment, care, moral rejuvenation and restoration disguised control, coercion and punishment. Stephen Humphries (1981) has documented the means by which birching, solitary confinement and dietary restrictions were administered, for example. Mary Carpenter in her evidence to the Select Committee on Criminal and Destitute Juveniles in 1852, emphasized the crucial importance of strict discipline: 'I would not object to really severe measures being resorted to if they were found necessary from the conduct of the child ... they must feel they are under positive and firm discipline' (quoted in Morris and Giller, 1987, p.29). Notwithstanding such practices, the means by which the institutions were positively presented is of crucial significance. It is important to understand the tendencies of institutional officials and policy-makers who insisted, and who continue to insist, upon giving the negative functions and practices of institutions a positive gloss, whether by presenting coercion as care or by packaging damaging punishment as constructive custody. We return to this point in section 4.3.

3.3   From institutional fix to fixed institution

Despite the concerns that we considered above, locked institutions for holding children have endured. Following on from the reformatories and industrial schools there have been: the borstals of the early twentieth century; the approved schools that were introduced in the 1930s; remand centres and detention centres established by the Criminal Justice Act 1948; Community Homes with Education ushered in by the Children and Young Persons Act 1969; secure accommodation which has developed and expanded since the 1970s and which awkwardly straddles the domains of child welfare, juvenile justice and child and adolescent mental health; the youth custody centres introduced in the early 1980s; the young offender institutions which emerged in the 1990s soon followed by the secure training centres (the first private jails for children); and the most recent incarnation of the locked institution is the detention and training centre (Goldson, 2002a).

Gill Stewart and Norman Tutt (1987, p.3) have observed that the numbers of children held in such places 'will vary over time, just as support or opposition to the expansion of secure facilities will vary with changes in social attitude and opinion'. Despite such fluctuation however, it is as 'normal' to have locked institutions for children in England and Wales as it is to have nurseries, schools or clinics. The locked institution has proved to be tenacious. It has become fixed – in its various forms – as a repository for the poorest and most disadvantaged children, and it comprises a seemingly indispensable linchpin of both 'welfare' (care) and 'justice' (control) systems. It is to the more contemporary context that our attention now turns: to the material conditions that frame the personal lives of children today; to the competing priorities of modern social policy; and to the experiences of children and staff within locked institutions.

4   Contemporary conditions, policies and practices

Although there have obviously been quite profound changes in socio-economic conditions, personal lives and social policies since the nineteenth century, many legacies have endured. Deeply rooted inequalities remain, policy-makers persevere in wrestling with questions of care and control, the child casualties of social injustice are still ascribed identities along the victim–threat continuum and locked institutions continue to operate at the deep end of the care–control complex.

4.1   Modern social policy and echoes of the past

Despite the fact that the UK boasts a relatively strong economy in the early part of the twenty-first century, inequality and poverty remain widespread. Furthermore, in some senses at least, as the economy gets stronger, inequality and poverty becomes more deeply embedded. For example, in relation to inequality, between 1979/1980 and 1999/2000 the growth in real income of the poorest 10 per cent of the UK population amounted to 6 per cent, which contrasts sharply with the staggering 86 per cent rise enjoyed by the richest 10 per cent over precisely the same twenty-year period (Child Poverty Action Group, 2002, p.4). Similarly, with regard to child poverty, in 1979/1980 1.4 million children – 10 per cent of all children in the UK – were living in poverty, but by 1999/2000 the corresponding figures had risen to 4.3 million children – 34 per cent of the total (DSS, 2001).

It was largely in response to such patterns of inequality and poverty that, in 1999, the Prime Minister Tony Blair stated that 'our historic aim will be for ours to be the first generation to end child poverty, and it will take a generation. It is a 20-year mission, but I believe it can be done' (quoted in Goldson, 2002d, p.687). Accordingly, the Labour Government set itself ambitious targets to end poverty and restore social justice for children. Such targets aimed to reduce child poverty by a quarter by 2004, halve it by 2010 and eradicate it completely by 2020. Although such anti-poverty statements are welcome, it is also important to understand that they are contingent and conditional. When impoverished children behave in such a way as to disturb moral sensibilities (what is increasingly termed 'anti-social behaviour'), or worse still to transgress the law, the humane logic of anti-poverty responses, generic child care priorities and broad based family support is eclipsed. It is at this very juncture that the institutional 'fix' is once again mobilized.

ACTIVITY 3.4

Contrast the tenor of the Prime Minister's 'historic pledge' statement – in respect of ending child poverty – which we referred to earlier, with the following quotation from the Labour Party manifesto document prepared for the 2001 General Election:

> We need a new approach to catch, convict, punish and rehabilitate more of them [child 'offenders'] ... persistent offending should lead to increased punishment ... firmer measures will be taken ... our proposals are based on a simple principle: stay straight or you will stay supervised or go inside.
>
> (Labour Party, 2001, p.33)

■ How do the two statements present different constructions of the disadvantaged child?

■ To what extent do they convey messages of care and control, victims and threats, deservingness and undeservingness?

COMMENT

In considering the statements you may have detected echoes of the nineteenth century. Steeped within the caring and compassionate sentiments underpinning the 'historic pledge', is the concept of the deserving child victim. This contrasts sharply with the controlling imperatives – 'increased punishment' and 'firmer measures' – that are directed at the child 'offender' who is perceived to be an undeserving threat. This is not the only remaining legacy of the nineteenth century however. As we noted at the conclusion of section 3.3, the locked institution has also endured. Furthermore, whereas such institutions are most commonly used for 'controlling' the 'threats' (in the way proposed in the statement above), they also continue to be deployed, albeit in a different guise, for 'caring' for 'victims'. In this way such institutions provide a residual service, a safety valve or backstop, reserved for children perceived either as *being at risk* or as *posing a risk*.

4.2 Modern institutions: controversy and paradox

Modern law and social policy in England and Wales provide two distinct routes along which children can be processed into specific types of locked institution. Therefore, children who are perceived as victims (for example, those who frequently run away from children's homes, children with self-harming tendencies, children who are abused and exploited as street prostitutes, mentally distressed children) can be 'placed' in *secure* accommodation. These secure units are managed by local authority social services departments and the Department of Health, and children are placed in them under the provisions of civil/child care statute (for example, the Children Act 1989). Alternatively, children who are regarded as threats (those charged with, or convicted of, offences) can be held on remand, or under sentence, in young offender institutions. These institutions are managed by the prison service and the Home Office, and children are detained in them in accordance with criminal justice legislation (for example, the Crime and Disorder Act 1998 and the Criminal Justice and Police Act 2001).

The vulnerabilities faced by children placed in secure accommodation under the provisions of civil/child care law and policy are considered to be so great that institutional confinement is sanctioned by the courts in order to keep them safe, promote their welfare and serve their 'best interests'. However, the rationale for placing children in young offender institutions is quite different. Here, it is the risk that children are thought to pose *to the community*, rather than the risks that they might experience *within it*, that applies. It follows that protection of the public takes precedence over protection of the child, and the withdrawal of liberty is legitimized by controlling rather than caring imperatives (Goldson, 2002c).

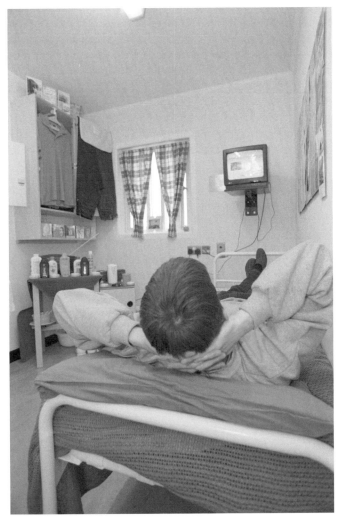

Figure 3.5   Interior of a modern young offender institution

ACTIVITY 3.5

Look carefully at Figure 3.5, a photograph of a child's room in a modern young offender institution, and jot down what you think are the characteristics of this room. Look back now at Figure 3.4, 'Bedtime at the reformatory at Mettray in France', and compare the different conditions experienced by children locked-up in the nineteenth century and those being held in young offender institutions at the beginning of the twenty-first century. Having noted the differences, can you think of ways in which the experiences of these children might be similar?

COMMENT

You may have noted that the child in the modern young offender institution has what appears to be a comfortably furnished room with access to a television and radio, as well as a number of personal possessions such as clothes, toiletries and cards. The nature of this space is clearly very different to the Mettray reformatory where the surroundings are bleak, uncomfortable and lacking in privacy. However, and despite these visible differences, the experiences of children at Mettray and those within modern young offender institutions have many similarities, not least because surveillance, regimentation and control have continued to structure institutional life over the past two hundred years. Despite some improvements in physical conditions, therefore, the varied practices of placing children in locked institutions continue to raise controversies and paradoxes.

For our purposes, five principal sources of controversy and paradox are particularly important in respect of secure accommodation and young offender institutions.

First, the practice of locking-up children in secure accommodation in order to care for them is deeply problematic and raises complex questions in relation to legal ethics, professional licence and human rights. Rachel Hodgkin has queried:

> Why exactly is it necessary to lock-up young people who are only a risk to themselves? What if their behaviour is untreatable within the locked placement? ... How can one determine which to lock-up of the many thousands of young people whose behaviours make them eligible for security? ... What filters, judicial or otherwise, ensure that only the necessary minimum are locked-up?
>
> (Hodgkin, 1995, p.7)

Such questions are particularly pertinent in relation to girls. Theresa O'Neill (2001) has observed that girls are more likely than boys to be contained in secure accommodation for reasons of 'care' and 'protection'; Annie Hudson (1989) has analysed the means by which girls' sexuality is problematized through constructions of 'promiscuity'; and Jim Wade et al. (1998) have researched the means by which social care agencies are significantly more inclined to employ institutional responses with girls who run away (and are thought to be in 'moral danger') than they are with boys. In other words, overtly gendered constructions of sexuality and adolescent behaviour can

serve to precipitate the restriction of liberty in respect of girls in [...]
not normally apply to boys. This resonates with the gender-specific [...]
that we discussed in section 3.2.

Second, there are both established and developing concerns relating to the
inhumane and often brutalizing conditions endured by children held in prison
service young offender institutions. Many children are so distressed by their
experiences that they deliberately harm themselves and/or attempt suicide
(Goldson, 2002c, pp.59–63). The paradox therefore, is that the locked
institution can be seen as comprising *relief from danger* for one identifiable
group of children (those in secure accommodation), and as a *source of danger*
for another (those in young offender institutions).

Third, of those children held in prison service young offender institutions, and
thus facing danger, black children are substantially over-represented and
racism is endemic within the wider youth justice system (Goldson and
Chigwada-Bailey, 1999; Goldson, 2002c). The 'corrosive disease' of racism
(Macpherson, 1999, para.6.34) not only means that black children are more
likely (than their white counterparts) to be held in such institutions, but they
also face the prospect of less favourable treatment and conditions when there.
The Director General of the Prison Service has recently acknowledged that the
prison system is 'institutionally racist' (quoted in Goldson, 2001, p.19), and
Her Majesty's Chief Inspector of Prisons has commented:

> I have long been concerned that the biggest single problem facing the Director
> General is the culture that still pervades parts of the prison system ... It is a culture
> that adopts an attitude to prisoners that is not only judgmental, but too often
> includes physical and mental brutality ... One of its most obvious manifestations is
> in attitudes to minorities ... whose inequality of treatment concerns me.
>
> (Her Majesty's Chief Inspector of Prisons, 2001, p.16)

Fourth, notwithstanding attempts at tidy conceptual differentiation between
child 'victims' and child 'threats', the children who are compartmentalized
within such constructions rarely, if ever, conform to exclusively victimized or
threatening identities and modes of behaviour. As we have seen, such
categorization serves to legitimize different forms of intervention organized
along a deserving–undeserving continuum, from caring welfarism to
controlling punitivism. The paradox is that the biographies of children
perceived as victims and those regarded as threats are almost always strikingly
similar. Research evidence repeatedly reveals the damaged backgrounds and
challenging social circumstances of both 'constituencies' of children. The
personal lives of such children typically comprise complex and layered
patterns of disadvantage including: social services involvement;
neighbourhoods beset by multiple and interlocking forms of deprivation;
families that have fractured and buckled under interminable pressure;
disrupted, incomplete, unhappy and relatively unproductive school careers;
poor health; unemployment, boredom and poverty; stunted opportunities and
unfulfilled aspirations; alienation and frustration; and abuse and exploitation
(Goldson, 2002c). As we noted earlier in this section, the system of locked

.ately comprises a residual repository for the containment of
dvantaged children.

rical claims that are made in order to legitimize the practices of
.ions continue to obfuscate their everyday operational realities.
.es of care and control become blurred through the presentation
.s care, and punishment as constructive custody. Such
ons can be seen to apply to secure accommodation and young
.stitutions. Official guidance issued by the Department of Health in
secure accommodation claims that it 'has an important role to play'
.asizes 'the specialist programmes which can be provided'. Moreover,
the s.. . guidance continues: 'it is important ... that there is a clear view of the
aims and objectives of such a placement and that those providing the
accommodation can fully meet those aims and objectives ... It is important that
plans are made for continuity of *care'* (DoH, 1993, para.8.5, emphasis added).
Secure accommodation is clearly legitimized within a discourse of care.
Similarly, the Youth Justice Board for England and Wales, acting on behalf of
the Home Office, issues national standards in relation to children in the prison
service's young offender institutions. While these institutions clearly seek
legitimacy by appealing to controlling imperatives, the official standards also
emphasize caring responsibilities: 'staff must undertake a reception interview
within one hour of the offender's [child's] arrival that assesses the offender's
needs and level of vulnerability' (Youth Justice Board, 2000, para.8.1.2,
emphasis added). Care and control overlap within the rhetoric of official
representation. For the child 'victim' *care demands control*, and for the child
'threat' *control demands care*.

With these paradoxes and controversies in mind, we conclude section 4 by
'testing' the rhetorical constructions of secure accommodation and young
offender institutions. By drawing upon primary research that gives voice to
children who are held in such institutions, and to staff who work in them
(Goldson, 2002c), we gain an insight into some of the realities of personal life
'inside'.

4.3   Personal lives inside: giving voice to children and staff in locked institutions

I undertook the research that underpins the remainder of section 4 over a 12-
month period in 2001 and 2002, and it investigated the complex and
interlocking vulnerabilities of children held in locked institutions. The
research was conducted in ten institutions (six secure units and four young
offender institutions) in England and data was gathered using a range of
methods including in-depth interviews. The interviewees included 40 children
who were being held in the institutions and 40 staff who worked within them.

Research of this nature raises complex ethical questions and highly charged
emotional responses and, in a chapter such as this, we do not have the space
to fully explore the breadth and depth of such issues. One such matter relates
to confidentiality and for this reason the quotations that follow are fully
anonymized. In presenting some of the research findings here, particular

attention is paid to constructions of care. Do the children and staff in secure accommodation experience and understand the practices of incarceration as expressions of care as the Department of Health guidance (quoted towards the end of section 4.2) suggests? Similarly, do the children and staff in young offender institutions feel that overtly controlling prison regimes also convey care, as the national standards state?

4.3.1 Inside secure accommodation

There is an extraordinarily limited pool of research available in relation to the effectiveness of secure accommodation. Although Roger Bullock and Michael Little (1991, p.2) have noted that 'there is little doubt that secure accommodation is an effective damper on the immediate [risk] posed by difficult behaviour or grave danger', little is known of the medium- to long-term effect. In posing the question, what is the effect of security on young people?, for example, Jenny Vernon (1995, p.2) concluded that 'despite the importance of this question, the relative absence of long-term studies means that there is a dearth of conclusive research evidence in this respect'.

We are more certain about the difficult and damaging circumstances that frame the personal lives of children placed in secure accommodation however, and in this sense it can be said to provide the 'immediate' relief to which Bullock and Little refer. Indeed, children and staff in secure accommodation appear to confirm this:

> If I hadn't come in here I could be dead now. I have a future ahead of me now. I had no future when I got in here. I have to think ahead now but before I just worked from day-to-day. That's the big difference. I've got a future now.
>
> (Girl, 15 years)

> It keeps them safe. It keeps them alive. It gives them an opportunity for reflection. It gives them an opportunity to be a child again.
>
> (Female secure unit staff)

In this sense, secure accommodation provides a caring sojourn facilitating immediate temporary relief from the dangers of the street: a safe enclosure, an opportunity to attend to primary health needs, a pit stop within which to restore a sense of 'childhood', a chance to rebuild emotional well-being and self-worth however fragile. This provides a rationale for the deprivation of liberty and it engenders a form of pragmatic acceptance for many members of staff. It neutralizes any sense of unease, it confirms their self-identities as caring people and it validates their role as carers:

> Young people are not secured on welfare grounds for singing out of tune in the choir. We do not secure children at the drop of a hat. The kids here are all at serious risk and if locking them up means that we can keep them safe then so be it.
>
> (Male secure unit staff)

Girls involved in child prostitution. We know they are the victims and it's the men who should be locked-up but we also know that things get worse unless there is an intervention and in order to address these issues they have to be in a safe environment. It can literally be a question of life and death, we have to keep them safe.

(Female secure unit staff)

I suppose that this is best explained by referring to specific examples. Take the young girl here at the moment, just 13 years old and heavily into child prostitution in London. We have to get kids like that safe and settled. How far can it be left to go before her life is lost either to adult control and abuse or literally lost? We have to help her to be a child again. Another example is serious self-harm issues. It seems ludicrous to lock such kids up but it can be the only way to keep them alive and to me that makes it legitimate. Many of these kids need us to take control. That sounds very punitive but it can be the only bloody way of keeping them alive.

(Female secure unit staff)

These comments illustrate the complexities of care and control that we have considered throughout this chapter. They also reveal crucial questions of power however, and some of these are neatly captured by the girl and the member of staff below:

I don't know. They've always told me that I'm vulnerable. They say I can't look after myself because of my age but age is nothing to do with it. Since the age of 11 I've been running off and looking after myself. When you're in care they don't care about you. That's their job but they're just there and you have to look after yourself. I'm not like a normal 15-year-old girl who has had a family and never run off. I've had to look after myself. OK I might have made mistakes and got into bad situations but it pisses me right off when they say I'm too young to look after myself. Who else will look after me because they won't? Some kids are vulnerable and some aren't. Some have been through more things and don't need to depend on others to help them. You learn as you go along how to do things, how to look after yourself, how to survive. When there is no-one else to look after you you've got to look after yourself so you
can't be vulnerable then can you?

(Girl, 15 years)

I worry about it all the time. For one you are locking a kid up who, although they have behaved in ways that worry us, has often not done anything strictly illegal, they have not harmed anyone else. You are touching on issues of human rights. They haven't done anything illegal but a magistrate deems that they need locking up for their own safety. For the kid it is their life and they think that they should be able to do what they want with it. It's very difficult really. A question that I ask myself is that as an adult if I did the same behaviour would I be locked-up for my own good. In most cases I wouldn't. It's a question of rights and who has the right to decide what is best. It is really difficult.

(Male secure unit staff)

- By drawing upon her personal life experience, what was this 15-year-old girl saying in relation to: care; the social construction of childhood; adult power; and state control?
- What questions is the male member of staff raising in relation to care and control?
- To what extent does his perspective overlap with that of the girl's?

In the two quotations, the very legitimacy of secure accommodation is problematized and contested. Both the girl and the member of staff challenge the power of courts and social services departments to define and intervene. The girl comments upon the failure of the formal child welfare system to care for her. Her maturational development and the pace of her personal life have been accelerated by circumstance. She has had to manage alone and this disturbs conventional constructions of the dependency of modern childhood. On this basis she resents the control imposed upon her by adult authority. Similarly, the member of staff fundamentally questions the basis of intervention. In instances when no criminal offence has been committed, when no harm to others has resulted, questions of moral sensibility alone can serve to violate human rights. The member of staff poses compelling questions in relation to the ethics of secure accommodation in such cases.

The temporary relief that secure accommodation provides is converted from a source of legitimacy to a site of major contestation. Its very temporariness is problematized. The contrived nature of interventions which deprive children of their liberty without addressing the wider social–structural conditions which serve to compromise their care, and undermine the quality of their personal lives, is profoundly questionable:

> If you're vulnerable and you come in here it isn't going to make you un-vulnerable is it? Just because I'm in here isn't going to change being vulnerable when I get out. I have to have help when I get out but it wasn't there when I came in and it probably won't be when I get out.
>
> (Girl, 14 years)

> We have kids and they make progress in a short while but their situations outside don't change. They're back to the same areas, the same streets, the same pressures, the same adults, the same peers. All of the same influences that got them in here in the first place.
>
> (Female secure unit staff)

Throughout the course of my interviews, children (and in many cases staff too) repeatedly emphasized the need for sustained and proactive care and support *responsive to needs* as distinct from *reactive to behaviour.* Notwithstanding all of the complexities therefore, the legitimacy of civil/care placements in secure accommodation – in many if not all cases – is open to question. Children face the prospect of deprived liberty because the wider social and economic system is unable or unwilling to meet their needs. Ultimately, such children are vulnerable not only to the perils of the street, but also to the damage imposed by poverty and inequality, to the failings of social policy, to the intrinsic neglect of the child care system, and to the excesses and misplaced application of adult power and state authority.

4.3.2 Inside young offender institutions

There is no shortage of evidence concerning the efficacy of prison service custody in relation to children. Such evidence is almost exclusively negative. Prison is expensive, damaging and counterproductive when measured against its own claims to reform and rehabilitate. Not only are post-release re-conviction rates extraordinarily high, but often the seriousness and gravity of offending is compounded following periods of custodial detention (Goldson and Peters, 2000). As Michel Foucault (1977, p.232) has perceptively noted 'prison ... is dangerous when it is not useless'. Notwithstanding the substantial weight of evidence however, the practice of confining children to various penal institutions has endured. As we have also noted however, in modern times the controlling and punitive functions of prison service institutions are increasingly given a rhetorical gloss of care. This particularly applies to the reception process (at the point of a child's arrival) where the care needs of children are meant to be assessed.

Her Majesty's Chief Inspector of Prisons (1997, p.28) explained that 'a positive start to his [sic] custodial experience is crucial for a young person, particularly a child. Reception is the area in which he first gains an impression of the establishment'. Similarly, three years later Her Majesty's Inspectorate of Prisons (2000, p.119) again emphasized 'the importance of sensitive treatment in reception', and the official national standards (that we referred to towards the end of section 4.2) also stress the importance of taking early account of the particular needs of child prisoners. Despite all of this however, the reality of reception practice is far removed from its rhetorical representation, as prison staff explain:

> More often than not, if I'm honest, I don't really interview them [children] properly at all. They don't want to discuss anything in front of anyone else. You just can't interview them at reception.
>
> (Male prison officer)

> If you are assessing vulnerability you need time. If they are coming into the prison late, which happens quite a lot, there is not enough time and they are going more or less straight behind the doors [into cells], so that staff can go home. It's all a case of getting the numbers into communications and getting the roll correct so that we can all go home. The whole prison is waiting for us, so people are rushing and not taking the adequate amount of time. It's a big bugbear. We are concerned that one of them is going to hang himself or self-harm and there will be a death on the wing. No-one likes to come across things like that.
>
> (Female prison officer)

Similarly, children explained their first contact with the young offender institutions in terms far removed from any notion of caring reception:

> It's really scary you don't know what to do and where to go. You have a little interview with an officer and a nurse and they ask if you're alright. I just said 'I'm alright' but I didn't really know if I was alright or not. I wasn't really listening to what they were telling me. I was really scared.
>
> (Boy, 16 years)

> The nurse asked if I had any medical problems and if I felt suicidal. I thought 'if they are asking me if I feel suicidal it must be horrible on the wings with loads of people killing themselves and they think I might kill myself'. They gave me a prison number and then I was just shoved on the wing.
>
> (Boy, 15 years)

> I just felt really alone and down. They just spoke to me like I was a piece of meat. They didn't make you feel like a person. I know I broke the law and that, but they just treated me like a piece of shit. They think 'cos you're in prison, and they're in uniform, they can just tell you to do what they want and treat you as bad as they want.
>
> (Boy, 16 years)

The words of the children express anything but the 'positive start' and 'sensitive treatment' to which the Chief Inspector of Prisons refers. There is little doubt that some prison staff try harder than others, and this too has been observed by the most senior prison inspector: 'some reception staff seem to be aware that the process is intimidating and potentially dehumanizing and adopt a suitably sensitive approach. Others seem not to understand this, to have become inured to it, or simply not to care' (Her Majesty's Inspectorate of Prisons, 2000, p.27). Irrespective of the levels of staff commitment however, the conditions within which children are received at prisons militate against any semblance of individual care. If the treatment and care of children at the point of reception is wanting, their experiences of 'doing time' is less favourable still. Some of the children reported particularly negative treatment from staff:

> Sometimes the way the officers speak to you is bad. They don't seem to care about you. I don't want to get them in trouble but I'm just speaking the truth. Honest, I'm just speaking the truth, they don't seem to care what happens to us lot in here.
>
> (Boy, 16 years)

But the situation is worse than this, and even if prison staff were willing and able to meet the care needs of children, staffing levels are clearly prohibitive:

> We don't give them enough basic care. They need more one-to-one support but we just don't give it, we can't with the numbers of staff to kids.
>
> (Female prison officer)

Let's face it, if you've got two or three staff on a wing with 65 kids, which is what we've got here at night, then how much support can you give them really?

(Male prison officer)

The consequences of such neglect for children are apparent:

It hurts all the time. All you do is miss your family and you can't hack it sometimes. I wouldn't send kids to a place like this.

(Boy, 16 years)

I felt very lonely and that, very lonely really. You are on your own and there is no-one to talk to. All you can do is think and it really winds you up. I had no-one to speak to and it all built-up and I started thinking that I can't take this anymore.

(Boy, 16 years)

Worse still, young offender institutions are not just neglectful, they are sites of concentrated bullying in all of its forms – physical assault, sexual assault, verbal abuse, racist abuse and assault, intimidation, extortion and theft. Prison staff explain:

It comes in waves, it depends who's on the wing. You get kids bullying each other, you get staff bullying kids and you get staff bullying staff. Some of us are deemed too soft. I talk to them as I talk to my own children. Other staff will say we're not strict enough in here because they're here for punishment, but we are not here to punish them further are we? Outside the kids can get status in lots of ways. In here status is measured in different ways: fear and respect become very confused. We tell them that we don't tolerate bullying at all, but they see it all around them. They won't tell you because that's grassing and it's a sin to grass. To be seen as a grass is seen as worse than putting up with the bullying. It comes with experience – seeing bullying, and then choosing how to deal with it. You'll never get rid of it though, it's power isn't it?

(Female prison officer)

I think that it occurs all the time in different ways: verbal and physical; prisoner to prisoner; staff to prisoner; and staff to staff. Especially with verbal bullying, or just an attitude which is a form of bullying, people don't always see it, particularly staff I would say. They call it discipline but it's really bullying, it's an abuse of power.

(Male prison nurse)

In other settings such behaviour would be called child abuse; in prison service institutions it is simply termed 'bullying'. However such behaviours and practices are described or explained, the experience of being bullied is always torturous and corrosive, and sometimes fatally so:

This lad gave me a half ounce of burn [tobacco] and said I had to pay him back a week later. I didn't know it was double back. He then wanted munch [crisps and biscuits] back too, and he kept on doubling it every week. He would shout through the window and threaten me and then everyone thought they can take me for a muppet [an easy target]. Every night they are shouting out the window, every single night, guaranteed. That's all you hear, that's all you hear every night.

(Boy, 16 years)

Every day, it goes on every day. You just see people who are quiet and they just get it all the time. When you come in here and you don't know anyone, you are just an easy target for bullies. They just see it as fun, but it's really bad if you are bullied, and some of them even commit suicide because of it.

(Boy, 15 years)

Every day, every day bullying happens. It's getting worser and worser. A kid has just killed himself and I reckon that was through bullying. A 16-year-old lad, a 16 year old does not kill themself when they have their whole life in front of them. I just picture it in my head and it's bad, it's really bad. It's all down to bullying, that's what it's all down to.

(Boy, 15 years)

Prison service institutions are not caring organizations despite the best efforts of many staff. They never have been, and they probably never will be. They cannot be. In the final analysis, and despite the rhetoric of care which seeks to blunt the punitive edge and claim legitimacy for the practices of child imprisonment, prisons are not supposed to be caring:

> Prisons collect [children] who find it difficult to cope, they collect excessive numbers of [children] with mental disorder, they collect [children] who have weak social supports, they collect [children] who, by any objective test, do not have rosy prospects. This collection of [children] is humiliated and stigmatized by the process of arrest, police inquiry and court appearance. [Child] prisoners suffer the ultimate ignominy of banishment to an uncongenial institution, which is often overcrowded, where friends cannot be chosen, and physical conditions are spartan. Above all, they are by the process separated from everything familiar, including all their social supports and loved ones, however unsatisfactory. This is what is supposed to happen, and this is what the punishment of prison is all about.

(Gunn quoted in Her Majesty's Chief Inspector of Prisons, 1999, p.25)

5   Conclusion

At the beginning of section 4 we noted that the past two hundred years have been witness to quite extraordinary social and economic changes, and few would doubt that the material quality of life in the UK has improved profoundly for the majority. However, we have also focused upon some core continuities which, taken together, begin to unsettle oversimplified concepts of progressive reform. Poverty and inequality continue to cut deep into the social fabric of UK society and state policy formation remains congealed around a familiar sequence of caring and controlling priorities. Ultimately however, care is located within a context of injustice, and injustice is policed by control as locked institutions continue to sweep up the casualties. Childhood is variously constructed, victim–threat identities are ascribed and the most 'appropriate' institutional responses are mobilized. Children within locked institutions – whether they be 'caring' or 'controlling' in nature – comprise a skewed population drawn from the most disadvantaged sections of society where class, 'race' and gender intersect and overlap in complex formations. The legitimacy for the continuing practices of locked institutions is invariably derived in rhetorical representations which serve to blur the boundaries of their caring and controlling functions. By giving voice to the children held in such institutions, together with the staff who work in them however, we have illuminated some of the complexities and contradictions of operational practices. The realities of personal lives inside rarely concur with the claims of neutralizing rhetoric.

We end where we began, by revisiting the United Nations Convention on the Rights of the Child (UNCRC). Formal ratification of the UNCRC obliges the government of each 'State party' to submit periodic reports (usually every five years) to the United Nations Committee on the Rights of the Child which is based in Geneva. The Committee then considers the detail of such reports, together with other evidence submitted by non-governmental organizations (NGOs), and assesses the extent to which policies and practices are consistent with the provisions of the UNCRC. In October 2002 the United Nations Committee formally responded to the most recent report submitted by the UK government. Two of the Committee's official observations are of particular significance for the purposes of our discussion:

> The Committee is extremely concerned at the high proportion of children living in poverty in the State party which limits their enjoyment of many rights under the Convention and leads to higher incidence among those children of mortality, accidents, teenage pregnancy, poor housing and homelessness, malnutrition, educational failures, or suicide. The Committee welcomes the State party's commitment to end child poverty and the initiative taken in this regard, but notes the lack of an effective and coordinated poverty eradication strategy across the State party.
>
> (United Nations Committee on the Rights of the Child, 2002, para.43)

> More generally, the Committee is deeply concerned at the high increasing numbers of children in custody ... Therefore, it is the concern of the Committee that deprivation of liberty is not being used only as a measure of last resort and for the shortest appropriate period of time, in violation of article 37(b) of the convention. The Committee is also extremely concerned at the conditions that children experienced in detention ... and that children do not receive adequate protection or help ... noting the very poor staff–child ratio, high levels of violence, bullying, self-harm and suicide.
>
> (United Nations Committee on the Rights of the Child, 2002, para.57)

Further resources

Few authors address the historical material that lies at the core of this chapter with as much authority as Hendrick (2003). Jones and Novak (1999) provide a comprehensive analysis of poverty and inequality, and Goldson et al. (2002) examine the specific impact of social injustice on children and young people. Kelly (1992) and Harris and Timms (1993) offer good overviews of secure accommodation, and Muncie et al. (2002) provide a penetrating critical assessment of contemporary youth justice. Government department websites contain a wealth of 'official' statistics and related publications, especially the Department of Health (http://www.doh.gov.uk), the Home Office (http://www.homeoffice.gov.uk) and Her Majesty's Inspectorate of Prisons (http://www.homeoffice.gov.uk/justice/prisons/inspprisons/index.html). (All these websites were last accessed on 15 July 2003.)

References

Bullock, R. and Little, M. (1991) *Secure Accommodation for Children*, Highlight no.103, London, National Children's Bureau and Barnardos.

Carpenter, M. (1851) *Reformatory Schools for the Children of the Perishing and Dangerous Classes and for Juvenile Offenders*, London, Gilpin.

Carpenter, M. (1853) *Juvenile Delinquents: Their Condition and Treatment*, London, Cash.

Child Poverty Action Group (2002) 'Poverty: the facts – summary', *Poverty*, no.111, pp.1–4.

Children's Rights Development Unit (1994) *The UK Agenda for Children*, London, Children's Rights Development Unit.

Cohen, S. (1985) *Visions of Social Control*, Cambridge, Polity Press.

DoH (Department of Health) (1993) *The Children Act 1989 Guidance and Regulations: Volume 4 Residential Care* (3rd impression), London, HMSO.

DSS (Department of Social Security) (2001) *Households Below Average Income*, London, HMSO.

Foucault, M. (1977) *Discipline and Punish*, London, Penguin.

Goldson, B. (2001) 'Behind locked doors: youth custody in crisis?', *Childright*, no.173, pp.18–9.

Goldson, B. (2002a) 'New punitiveness: the politics of child incarceration' in Muncie et al. (eds) (2002).

Goldson, B. (2002b) 'Children, crime and the state' in Goldson et al. (eds) (2002).

Goldson, B. (2002c) *Vulnerable Inside: Children in Secure and Penal Settings*, London, The Children's Society.

Goldson, B. (2002d) 'New Labour, social justice and children: political calculation and the deserving-undeserving schism', *British Journal of Social Work*, vol.32, no.6, pp.683–95.

Goldson, B. and Chigwada-Bailey, R. (1999) '(What) justice for black children and young people?' in Goldson, B. (ed.) *Youth Justice: Contemporary Policy and Practice*, Aldershot, Ashgate.

Goldson, B., Lavalette, M. and McKechnie, J. (eds) (2002) *Children, Welfare and the State*, London, Sage.

Goldson, B. and Peters, E. (2000) *Tough Justice: Responding to Children in Trouble*, London, The Children's Society.

Harris, R. and Timms, N. (1993) *Secure Accommodation in Child Care: Between Hospital or Prison or Thereabouts?*, London, Routledge.

Hendrick, H. (1994) *Child Welfare: England 1872–1989*, London, Routledge.

Hendrick, H. (2003) *Child Welfare: Historical Dimensions, Contemporary Debate*, Bristol, The Policy Press.

Her Majesty's Chief Inspector of Prisons (1997) *Young Prisoners: A Thematic Review by HM Chief Inspector of Prisons for England and Wales*, London, Home Office.

Her Majesty's Chief Inspector of Prisons (1999) *Suicide is Everyone's Concern: A Thematic Review by HM Chief Inspector of Prisons for England and Wales*, London, Home Office.

Her Majesty's Inspectorate of Prisons (2000) *Unjust Deserts: A Thematic Review by HM Chief Inspector of Prisons of the Treatment and Conditions for Unsentenced Prisoners in England and Wales*, London, Her Majesty's Inspectorate of Prisons for England and Wales.

Her Majesty's Chief Inspector of Prisons (2001) *Report of Her Majesty's Chief Inspector of Prisons December 1999–November 2000*, London, Home Office.

Hodgkin, R. (1995) *Safe to Let Out? The Current and Future Use of Secure Accommodation for Children and Young People*, London, National Children's Bureau.

Hudson, A. (1989) '"Troublesome girls": towards alternative definitions and policies' in Cain, M. (ed.) *Growing Up Good: Policing the Behaviour of Girls in Europe*, London, Sage.

Humphries, S. (1981) *Hooligans or Rebels?*, Oxford, Basil Blackwell.

Jones, C. and Novak, T. (1999) *Poverty, Welfare and the Disciplinary State*, London, Routledge.

Jenks, C. (1996) *Childhood*, London, Routledge.

Kelly, B. (1992) *Children Inside: Rhetoric and Practice in a Locked Institution for Children*, London, Routledge.

Labour Party (2001) *Ambitions for Britain*, London, Labour Party.

Lewis, G. (1998) *Forming Nation, Framing Welfare*, London, Routledge in association with The Open University.

Macpherson, Sir William (1999) *The Stephen Lawrence Inquiry: Report of an Inquiry by Sir William Macpherson of Cluny*, Cmnd 4262–1, London, The Stationery Office.

May, M. (1973) 'Innocence and experience: the evolution of the concept of juvenile delinquency in the mid nineteenth century' in Muncie et al. (eds) (2002).

Morris, A. and Giller, H. (1987) *Understanding Juvenile Justice*, London, Croom Helm.

Muncie, J., Hughes, G. and McLaughlin, E. (eds) (2002) *Youth Justice: Critical Readings*, London, Sage.

Novak, T. (2002) 'Rich children, poor children' in Goldson et al. (eds) (2002).

O'Neill, T. (2001) *Children in Secure Accommodation: A Gendered Exploration of Locked Institutional Care for Children in Trouble*, London, Jessica Kingsley.

Saraga, E. (ed.) (1998) *Embodying the Social: Constructions of Difference*, London, Routledge in association with The Open University.

Scraton, P. (ed.) (1997) *'Childhood' in 'Crisis'?*, London, UCL Press.

Shamgar-Handelman, L. (1994) 'To whom does childhood belong?' in Qvortrup, J. (ed.) *Childhood Matters: Social Theory, Practice and Politics*, Aldershot, Avebury.

Shore, H. (2002) 'Reforming the juvenile: gender, justice and the child criminal in nineteenth-century England' in Muncie et al. (eds) (2002).

Stewart, G. and Tutt, N. (1987) *Children in Custody*, Aldershot, Avebury.

United Nations Committee on the Rights of the Child (2002) *Concluding Observations of the Committee on the Rights of the Child: United Kingdom of Great Britain and Northern Ireland*, Geneva, United Nations.

Vernon, J. (1995) *En Route to Secure Accommodation*, London, National Children's Bureau.

Wade, J., Biehal, N., Clayden, J. and Stein, M. (1998) *Going Missing: Young People Absent from Care*, Chichester, John Wiley.

Wright, E.O. (1979) *Class, Crisis and the State*, London, Verso.

Youth Justice Board (2000) *National Standards for Youth Justice*, London, Youth Justice Board for England and Wales.

CHAPTER 4

Skin Matters: 'Race' and Care in the Health Services

by Yasmin Gunaratnam

Contents

1   Introduction

As we have seen in Chapter 1, care as a concept and a practice has very different individual and social meanings that are related to the identities of those who need care and those who give care, and where care relationships take place. Drawing upon these central themes of meanings, identities and sites of practice, this chapter extends our explorations of care through a focus upon how the relationships between 'race', ethnicity and care are given meaning in individual accounts of intercultural care in the health services. By looking at how we can interpret personal narratives in ways that are attentive to local and broader contexts, the chapter uses 'the personal' to map how racialized relationships of care are produced and have unexpected connections across diverse experiences and social spaces.

The chapter examines these connections through one account of care in an English hospice ward, narrated in a group discussion by 'Gill' (a pseudonym), a white British hospice nurse, during my ethnographic research in a London hospice. In the account, Gill talks about her professional and personal dilemmas in caring for a Ugandan woman dying with AIDS dementia, and raises concerns about how ethnicity, language difference and disease may have affected communication and the quality of care that the woman received. In addition to highlighting professional and personal dilemmas, Gill's account reflects key areas of concern in current policy discourses and in service development in the health care services that relate to questions of institutional racism in public sector services and the need for 'culturally competent' care.

The sites of the professional, the interpersonal and the institutional that are implicated in Gill's account are clearly important in understanding how care can become racialized. However, an argument that is pivotal to this chapter is that, in order to gain meaningful insights into the relationships between personal lives and social policy, we have to connect the intensely located nature of 'the personal' to broader contexts. This argument has particular meanings in addressing 'race' and ethnicity in postcolonial contexts, where the transnational and historical movement of people, things and ideas has meant that there are always relationships of power between the past and the present and the local and the global.

To examine these connections in interpreting Gill's account, our analysis will move beyond the local site of the hospice and the unique microdynamics of the interaction that she describes, to explore how Gill's dilemmas might be related to very different experiences and to wider social processes. These connections will be made through a 'multi-sited' (Marcus, 1998) analysis of Gill's account. Such an analysis is based upon the recognition that any account or interaction is never fully enclosed within a particular cultural domain, but is produced through conditions that are always both 'here and there' (Marcus, **multi-sited** 1998, p.117). Interpretation in **multi-sited analysis** pushes us to move **analysis** outwards from any narrative and site, in order to map and make visible how a narrative/interaction is linked to other settings and social arrangements.

My analysis of Gill's account will thus move across different individual experiences and social contexts that include my own positioning within the research process. In this sense, the chapter is also an invitation to journey across different personal lives. Despite this invitation, I am not offering an 'easy' ride. In using 'the personal' to zigzag through the spaces of localized professional–service user interactions, research relationships, knowledge production and global bio-political relationships, the discussion aims to work against a passive reading and consumption of 'the personal'. Rather, 'the personal' will be used to ask questions about how we as individuals might be located within wider systems of racialized power and oppression and how we might use 'the personal' to make sense of, to testify to, and to transform oppressive practices and discourses.

Aims The aims of the chapter are to:

- Examine how we might interpret personal narratives of intercultural care in the health services in ways that provide insight into wider social and historical processes.

- Look at care in relation to professional practices, and to analytic practice and the production of knowledge and understanding.

- Provide an example of how multi-sited approaches to research and analysis can be of benefit to a social policy that is concerned with personal lives.

The chapter is structured around five main areas:

1 a detailing of my approach to the notion of 'the personal' and to care;

2 an overview of hospices as sites of care and their relationships to wider policy discourses and professional education approaches to intercultural care;

3 an examination of the racialized dynamics of care through an account of intercultural care from Gill, a white British hospice nurse;

4 attention to the connections between postcolonial relationships and a multi-sited analysis;

5 the application of a multi-sited analysis to Gill's account.

2 Underlying concepts: 'the personal' and care

Before we explore the relationships between personal lives and social policy in the context of 'race', ethnicity and hospice care, it is important to make clear some of the conceptual ideas that underlie the discussions in the chapter. In this section I look at how I have conceptualized 'the personal', and discuss my approach to the process of analysing individual accounts drawn from my **ethnographic research** in an English hospice, which elaborates upon my conceptualization of care as an analytic practice.

ethnographic research

During the hospice research, conducted between 1995 and 1999, I worked alongside staff as a volunteer in the hospice day centre and accompanied hospice 'home-care' nurses as a non-participating observer on home visits to service users. The research included 33 interviews with 23 service users from South-Asian, African and Caribbean backgrounds, and 14 group interviews with different professionals (nurses, doctors, social workers and members of the chaplaincy team). The hospice staff I interviewed at the time of the research were predominantly white English women.

For the purposes of this discussion, the term 'ethnographic' is used to refer to an approach to research, that, as Skeggs has described, involves:

> fieldwork that will be conducted over a *prolonged period of time*, utilizing different research techniques; conducted *within the settings* of the participants, with an understanding of how the context informs the action; *involving the researcher in participation* and observation; involving an account of the development of relationships between the researcher and the researched and focusing on how experience and practice are part of wider processes.
>
> (Skeggs, 2001, p.426, original emphasis)

Skeggs's references to the need for researchers to have an understanding of how the wider context can inform localized actions, and to the importance of accounts of the relationships between the researcher and research participant(s) within the research process are of specific relevance to an understanding of ethnography. These points are also relevant with regard to my conceptualization of care as an analytic practice and relate to how, as researchers, we produce accounts of research, and how, as researchers and readers, we interpret personal narratives. In this sense, the chapter is concerned with care practices at two levels: as a professional practice within the health services and as a practice of interpretation and understanding that involves a commitment to uncovering and making sense of power relationships and the intersections between 'the personal' and the social.

2.1 'The personal'

In the following discussion, I have conceptualized 'the personal' as involving the simultaneous ontological and discursive dimensions of identity and experience. That is, 'the personal' is approached as a lived, fleshy, felt

ontological experience

experience of being in the world – an **ontological experience** in which emotions and bodily states are critical areas of consideration. 'The personal' is also approached as an experience that is produced through, and which produces, discourses or 'sets of organized meanings' (Hollway and Jefferson, 2000, p.14).

My concern with the discursive elements of 'the personal' relates to how identities are continually brought to life and are negotiated, moment by moment, in everyday interactions. This emphasis upon identities as being actively given meaning and substance by individuals is an important one. It means that, rather than seeing 'race' and ethnicity as 'natural' categories of identity into which individuals are born and whose meanings are pre-given and anchored, we approach them as dynamic processes of being (Lewis, 1998). With this conceptual approach to social identities, we cannot prejudge what it means to be a Ugandan woman with AIDS, or a white English woman hospice nurse. Instead, assumptions are replaced with an open questioning of categories. In this discussion, for instance, I will ask how the categories of 'Ugandan', 'woman' and 'with AIDS' and the categories of 'nurse', 'English', 'woman' and 'white' are given meaning within talk about an English hospice ward, by whom and when. I ask questions about the relationships between the different categories of identity, and I also question what interpersonal and social effects the situated meanings of these categories have.

ACTIVITY 4.1

Make a note of your different identities and map how they relate to each other using the following questions as a guide:

- Which identities (social or organizational) give you some, if any, power? In which contexts? And with whom?

- How might your different identities affect any of the interactions that you have or have had in or with the health services?

Through the analysis of the hospice accounts I demonstrate how questioning the meanings of categories of identity and problematizing the fixing of divisions between identities – such as divisions between 'scholars' and 'practitioners', 'insiders' and 'outsiders', and 'white' and 'black' – are critical in the process of developing less abstract and more sensitive approaches to a diverse range of lived experiences.

Questions that I would like you to think about in making sense of the personal narratives that are used in this chapter are:

- What categories of identity are produced within the accounts, and how?

- What are the relationships between different identities?

- How do the individual accounts relate to the identities of the speaker and to broader interactional, organizational and social contexts?

2.2   Care as an analytic practice

In addition to the care that is needed in producing and interpreting personal narratives, analytic care takes on particular meanings when we are seeking to engage with questions of 'race' and ethnicity. Here, I am referring to how practices of interpretation can be used to gain insights into the complicated meanings of 'race' and ethnicity within postcolonial contexts, enabling us at the same time to examine how research is positioned within such contexts. I see the multi-sited approach that I use to analyse the hospice accounts later on in the chapter as a 'caring' analysis because it is able to address these two entangled relationships. It recognizes postcolonial relationships as involving both literal and symbolic border crossings that necessitate a chasing and mapping of meanings across social spaces. At the same time, rather than seeing research as a practice that 'objectively' reflects a local reality, it sees research as embedded in discourses and experiences that are localized but which are connected to other contexts, without it always being clear what these other contexts are (Marcus, 1998, p.119).

What characterizes multi-sited approaches to research is that uncertainty about the relationships between the local and an 'elsewhere' is seen as producing levels of 'curiosity' and 'anxiety' in both the researcher and the research participant (Marcus, 1998, p.122). The challenge for the researcher/reader – and what draws the analysis away from a single focus – is to recognize and explore how personal narratives and interactions are concerned with, and enmeshed in, what is happening outside the research relationship. So, in multi-sited analyses, affinities between researchers and research participants – no matter how different they are – are recognized and cared about and are seen as analytic clues that can tell us something about how the research encounter is positioned and oriented towards other contexts. The recognition of a relationship of involvement between the research participant and the researcher has been called '**complicity**' by Marcus (1998) and has been seen as vital in making connections between 'the personal' and the social.

complicity

Taken together, the different points that I have made about the particular value of using a multi-sited analysis to understand racialized relationships of care through personal narratives can be summarized as follows:

- It can be used to interpret localized accounts in ways that provide insights into broader lived experiences and institutional and social discourses and practices, enabling us to move backwards and forwards between 'the personal', the interpersonal and wider contexts. In this discussion, for example, you will see how my concern with my research encounter with Gill, will take my analysis to very different social and interactional contexts.

- Its engagement with the circulation and mobility of people, social processes and discourses, in contemporary postcolonial environments, is particularly suited to examining the complicated meanings and effects of practices that categorize people through 'race' (practices of **racialization**).

racialization

reflexivity

- Its attention to the importance of research relationships demands the use of **reflexivity** by the researcher, as a practice of making explicit and relevant the researcher's embodied social and interactional positioning within the research. Research dynamics can then be opened to scrutiny and the reader can be more able to see and judge how the research relationship is interactionally and socially located.

As the discussion moves on, I continue to consider the production, interpretation and understanding of individual accounts of care. By keeping these issues in mind, I hope to bridge the distances between my concerns with care as a professional practice and care as an analytic practice. You are encouraged to reflect upon and question these relationships as the discussion develops. How can accounts of professional care that are generated in highly specific contexts, for example, be used to understand broader social processes? Why is it important to consider the interpersonal and local contexts in which qualitative research accounts are produced in making judgements about the relationships between research and an 'elsewhere'? What are the consequences for our understanding of accounts of care when our analysis is also concerned with the dynamics of qualitative research relationships?

3   Hospices, cultural competence and care

intercultural
hospice care

In order to contextualize our discussion of Gill's account of **intercultural hospice care**, this section provides an overview of hospices and moves on to look at professional nurse education and training initiatives on intercultural care.

3.1   Hospices, difference and care

Hospices provide care for people with terminal and, more recently, chronic illnesses and disease, and have been seen as constituting 'a significant landmark in modern health care provision' (Clark, 1993, p.3). The first modern hospice, St Christopher's in South London, was founded outside of the National Health Service (NHS) in the late 1960s. By 2002 there were 208 hospice and palliative care services in the UK (Hospice Information, 2002). Hospices are a part of the voluntary sector (Clark, 1993). They receive financial support from the NHS but significant levels of funding can come from charitable and voluntary donations, and trained volunteers are often involved in a range of hospice activities including fund-raising, bereavement counselling and service-user support.

holistic care

Hospice care has been seen as subverting the traditional biomedical focus upon physical care needs through the promotion of models of '**holistic care**' that aim to take account of the physical, emotional, spiritual and social needs of service users. This holistic approach to care can be seen in hospice approaches to pain: 'Pain was not just a physical sensation: it might be a consequence of loneliness, spiritual distress, inappropriate diet, or tumour growth. Careful listening was the important skill in determining the best way to reduce patient discomfort' (Sielbold, 1992, p.16).

Despite their innovative approaches, the development of hospice care has been marked by a series of contradictory dynamics and tensions. A particular area of tension lies in the commitment of hospices to the recognition of difference and diversity in their philosophies of individually tailored holistic care, and what is seen as the exclusive and ethnocentric nature of hospice service provision and staffing. For example, a strong theme in representations of the historical evolution of hospice care is the construction of hospices as a social 'movement', involving 'leaders' and 'participants' whose actions have been directed at influencing wider cultural changes (Sielbold, 1992). Key characteristics of the hospice 'movement' have been identified as its charismatic leadership, a narrowness of focus and a highly committed, socially homogeneous (often described as being 'white, middle-class and Christian')

Figure 4.1   Hospices have promoted models of holistic care

and visible group of founder members (James and Field, 1992). During my hospice research in the mid-1990s, hospices were coming under growing critique and scrutiny both nationally (Hill and Penso, 1995) and internationally (Brenner, 1997) for their social exclusiveness.

ACTIVITY 4.2

Read through the recommendations on care, given in Extract 4.1 below. These recommendations were made in 2001 in a report entitled *Wider Horizons* (Firth, 2001) by the National Council of Hospice and Specialist Palliative Care Services (NCHSPCS). The report produced seven pages of recommendations. I have picked out four that cover the main areas highlighted in the section on 'Care issues'.

As you read the extract, consider the following questions:

■   What issues are being flagged as important for the provision of intercultural hospice care?

■   Do these recommendations suggest that the report extended initiatives to promote 'race' equality in the health services?

> ### Extract 4.1   *Wider Horizons*: recommendations
>
> - hospitals and hospices need to provide culturally sensitive palliative care with adequate interpreting/advocacy services, a culturally sensitive disclosure policy [here disclosure is referring to telling service users about a terminal diagnosis], and adequate discharge policies. This involves on-going in-service training in anti-discrimination as well as cultural competence;
> - dietary and religious requirements should be discussed fully with users on an individual basis, so that there is provision for special needs, including water for ablutions, prayer time/space, skin, hair and hygiene needs and appropriate clothing or gowns for patients;
> - ethnic minority staff should be recruited where possible, and advocates/interpreters made readily available;
> - anti-racism and anti-discrimination policies have to be firmly established and met at all levels of care, including protection from racist patients; ...
>
> (Firth, 2001, p.92)

COMMENT

In reading through the recommendations from the *Wider Horizons* report, you may have noticed that the issues highlighted, such as **cultural sensitivity** and competence, language and advocacy provision, dietary and religious requirements and the specific need for service providers to recruit 'ethnic minority' staff, are not new. These issues have characterized discussions of 'race' equality in the health services for a number of years (see Ahmad, 1993) and are still prominent today (see Figure 4.2). Cultural 'sensitivity' and 'competence', and the statutory duty upon public agencies to promote 'race' equality (Race Relations (Amendment) Act 2000) are now central to policy and service development initiatives and to debates on professional care in the health services (Alexander, 1999; Department of Health, 2000).

cultural sensitivity

---

cultural competence

With particular regard to nursing care, the need for training and education in '**cultural competence**' has been a recurring theme in policy discussions (Alexander, 1999; Firth, 2001), professional organizations (English National Board For Nursing, Midwifery and Health Visiting, 1990) and within the nurse education literature (Gerrish et al., 1996; Papadopoulos et al., 1998). By examining professional nurse education and training initiatives in more detail, we will see how they are important sites of analysis in making sense of Gill's account of intercultural care that is discussed in section 4.

3.2   Nurse education and training in cultural competence

When we look at popular approaches to the skills and knowledge that nurses are seen as needing in order to be culturally competent, it is apparent that

Figure 4.2   Equality in service provision in the NHS has been linked with the need for a more diverse workforce

approaches struggle with the need to 'contextualize the health experiences of minority ethnic communities within the broader social and political arena' (Gerrish et al., 1996, p.5) and the need for nurses to have specific '**cultural**

cultural knowledge

knowledge' (Papadopoulos et al., 1998) of different ethnic groups. Gerrish et al. (1996), in a study examining the preparation of nurses and midwives in England to work in multi-ethnic contexts, have made distinctions in ways of working with these tensions in developing cultural competence in nursing. Using the work of Kim (1992) on cross-cultural communication, Gerrish et al. conceptualize cultural competence as needing to involve specific skills of 'cultural communicative competence' and more generic skills of 'intercultural communicative competence'.

By 'cultural communicative competence', the authors are referring to the more task-oriented requirement for nurses to 'learn to understand the cultural values, behavioural patterns and rules for interaction in specific cultures' (Gerrish et al., 1996, p.26). The more process-oriented need for nurses to be open and adaptable in their care practices is reflected in the notion of 'intercultural communicative competence'. Drawing upon earlier work by Kim (1989), Gerrish et al. (1996, p.28) suggest that there are three dimensions of intercultural communicative competence through which rigidity can be avoided and openness to difference can be pursued:

1   The *cognitive* – 'The cognitive dimension ... is a creative flexibility in one's thought processes. It is a refusal to be dogmatic, or to insist on reducing new experiences to familiar or safe categories of understanding.'

2   The *affective* is seen as relating to emotions and can be positive – 'an emotional openness to others' – or negative, marked by threat and an 'inner-directed, protective setting of boundaries', or both.

3   The *behavioural* is conceptualized as the ability to express the insights that are generated in the cognitive and the affective in action – 'the behavioural dimension is all about our ability to adapt and be flexible in new situations.'

Gerrish et al.'s examination of cultural competence in nursing is innovative in the sense that it applies models of holistic care to practitioners. It recognizes nurses as whole people, and highlights the need for training and education to address nurses' thoughts, experiences and emotions in intercultural encounters. If we look more closely at the authors' promotion of culturally specific knowledge and the need for training in transferable and generic intercultural skills, however, we can see how this recognition of emotions is a contradictory one.

At one level the authors recognize intercultural interactions as encounters that can be characterized by emotions provoked by anticipation of threat for practitioners, due to possibilities of 'things going wrong' (Gerrish et al., 1996, p.30) and practice being rendered incompetent. This recognition is valuable in examining unconscious emotions such as fear and anxiety, and in addressing the contradictions between thoughts, emotions and practice. Yet, the approach of Gerrish et al. does not fully engage with the implication of these themes of emotion and is based upon a largely rationalist model of subjectivity. Drawing upon arguments made by Hollway and Jefferson (2000, pp.11–12), I would argue that the nurse who is assumed in Gerrish et al.'s approach to culturally competent care is one who:

■   is a 'rational actor', who with the right information, training and
     supervision can provide culturally sensitive and anti-discriminatory care;

■   is knowledgeable about, and can control his or her actions, emotions and
     feelings;

■   can process relevant information and guidance and apply it to his or her
     practice;

■   is capable of rationally evaluating his or her own practice.

These underlying assumptions of the subjectivity of nurses can also be seen in
resources designed to support the acquisition of cultural knowledge by
practitioners, and have been marked by what I have called the 'fact-file'
approach (Gunaratnam, 1997). Such resources involve the cataloguing of
information on the cultural and religious practices of different groups
racialized as being 'minority ethnic', where specific attention is given to
practices and rituals surrounding key life events such as births and deaths (for
examples see Green, 1991, 1992). The rationale behind the resources is that
increased 'cultural knowledge' – an understanding of the values and cultural
prescriptions operating within a service user's culture – can lead to greater
cultural sensitivity and competence in care (Papadopoulos et al., 1998).
Cultural 'fact-file' approaches have been based upon providing nurses with
generalized descriptions of the behaviours and attitudes of different ethnic and
religious groups. Extract 4.2 provides an example.

> ### Extract 4.2   'General considerations for the living'
>
> Muslims attach great importance to cleanliness. Hands, feet and mouth are
> always washed before prayer, and after menstruation women are required to
> wash their whole bodies. In hospital the use of a shower rather than a bath will
> be appreciated.
>
> Muslim women may prefer to be seen or treated by a female doctor, and
> consideration should be given to their modesty if requested.
>
> Most Muslims are accustomed to having water in the same room as the toilet. If
> a bedpan has to be used, then a bowl of water should also be provided for
> washing.
>
> (Green, 1991, p.2)

Two important analytic considerations are, first, how such approaches to the
education and training needs of professionals serve to produce the meanings
of racialized care; and, second, how they relate to lived experiences of
intercultural care. As we have seen, the rhetoric of cultural competence,
particularly as it relates to the need for nurses to have 'cultural knowledge',
can treat culture and racialized difference as discrete, identifiable conditions,
not unlike medical conditions, that can be observed, categorized, and
'treated'/mastered by practitioners. The limitations of such 'culturalist'
approaches are that they can serve to freeze or 'reify' the dynamic and
changing nature of the meanings of 'race' and ethnicity in lived experience.

And they can serve to define and reduce needs and experiences primarily to 'race', ethnicity and/or religion, thereby failing to engage with how other forms of social difference (such as gender, class and age) and unique biographical differences can affect individual meanings of 'race' and ethnicity.

There can also be significant gaps between the policy-driven quantitative equalities frameworks, dominated by the setting of standards, targets, competencies and output indicators, in which care is monitored in relation to wider performance management systems (Khan, 2001) and the emotional nature and content of care practices (Gunaratnam and Lewis, 2001). My reference to the emotional nature of care practices in this context is different from Gerrish et al.'s (1996) recognition of the affective dimensions of cultural competence, in that it involves the recognition of unconscious and irrational emotions. This psychodynamic approach to subjectivity assumes levels of an unconscious defensiveness, in which individuals can be motivated not to know certain things about themselves, and can act and produce accounts of their actions/experiences in ways which avoid such knowledge.

In the next section, we look at Gill's account of intercultural care, and examine further how attention to unconscious emotion is valuable in understanding the limitations of current approaches to racialized care and in making sense of the gaps between policy and practice. This discussion will provide an example of care as an analytic practice that seeks to connect the local and wider social, psychic, institutional and professional contexts.

4   Intercultural hospice care: Gill's account

Extract 4.3 below is taken from a group interview with four white British hospice nurses. The extract flows around an account by Gill of her experiences of caring for a Ugandan woman with AIDS.

ACTIVITY 4.3

You will need to read through Extract 4.3 at least a couple of times to grasp something of the complex nature of the care dilemmas that Gill talks about. As you read through the extract, explore as honestly as you are able to your own emotional and interpretive responses to the extract, including noting those areas of feeling that are expressed in the form of a mood or image rather than a word or sentence.

In generating your own interpretations, you might find it helpful to think about the following questions:

■   What do Gill and the other nurses find particularly challenging about providing care for the Ugandan woman?

■   How is whiteness made visible and given meaning within the discussion?

Extract 4.3   From a group interview with hospice nurses

Gill: I was just thinking about this one lady in particular. I found it extremely hard to get alongside her. I would say because of the cultural differences I would think, um, but I'm not sure, there was a lot to her case in particular, but, I feel that with, here, we do get alongside patients and we are very good at that. Very good at getting to know them ... and caring for them, but this, er, I found it with Ugandan women in particular actually, that I find it very difficult to, to I suppose read them. You know, I suppose I go a lot on people's non-verbals as well as what they say, and when the language is different you go a lot on people's non-verbals. And when you're faced with somebody who's Ugandan, who their very culture, you know, er sort of suppresses facial features, you know and they've got a very flat face, um (long pause).

Yasmin: A non-expressive face?

Gill: Yes. Yeah. I'm trying to think of the right word, but yes that's what I mean. But that was coupled with slowed mental processes from dementia. So it was very difficult, but I found we never really got alongside her ... I suppose I view that as a failure of care in a way ... but then can you, can we ever, as somebody from a completely different culture, you know that's what I find interesting, is can I, could I ever have done that you know, given more time? Because there was you know, there, it's in-bred in, it was in-bred in her not to er, divulge much information, which you know, she didn't want us to get to know her. So you know I don't know really (laughs).

Roz: Yes ... if that was me, as a nurse I would be really worrying that I hadn't done my best by that person ... and was it ... because I was white and hadn't a clue about her background? Whether that was what held me up?

Kate: Yeah, but some patients ... wherever they're from

(interjects)

Roz: Yeah, are really private

(interjects)

Kate: Go in on themselves when they're dying and have to find (pause) the strength from within, which means they don't speak

(interjects)

Roz: I think it's a feeling that you might have failed them ... that for me is quite hard, cause I think 'well, as a nurse I'm here cause I want to be useful' and somebody is very private then you can't be ... So is that me having a problem because I haven't achieved, 'cause I want the sort of kick I want to get out of nursing? Or has indeed that person missed out on something that, that they would have found useful? Or that in other circumstances, with other people they would have accessed?

COMMENT

There are a number of immediate questions that are provoked by Gill's account and which relate to the meanings that she gives to caring across racialized difference: How real is the 'race' seen and felt in the distance between Gill and the Ugandan woman in this English hospice ward? Could things have been different given more time? Could the woman have received better care if Gill was more knowledgeable about Ugandan culture? Or might better care have been provided by a black Ugandan nurse from a similar cultural background? Is this 'simply' a failure of cross-cultural communication and care, or an inevitable result of unbridgeable racialized difference, complicated by language difference and AIDS dementia?

In examining the extract more closely we can see that the racialized difference between Gill and the Ugandan woman is produced in two main ways that centre upon Gill's construction of 'in-bred' difference. On one axis of meaning, biological and cultural notions of difference are called up through 'race' and ethnicity to produce 'Ugandanness' as a distinct and separate experience of being from that of the nurses and their understanding of themselves as white. On another axis, any gendered connections between Gill and the Ugandan woman are eclipsed by 'race' and its associations with AIDS, so that the 'otherness' of the woman is given meaning primarily through disease and its interrelationships with 'race', ethnicity and culture. Gill's interpretation of gendered Ugandanness as an 'in-bred' subjectivity, embodied and observed in the empty 'flat face' of difference that stares back at her, is given added authority by Gill's reference to her cultural knowledge and experience of all the Ugandan women she has nursed. Hence, the category of 'Ugandan women' is produced as other, 'they are not the same as us' and as an undifferentiated and homogeneous one, 'they are all the same'. By positioning herself as 'somebody from a completely different culture' Gill implicitly constructs her own whiteness as the norm both in the context of her work on an English hospice ward and in the ease with which she is able to engage in relationships of care. However, the authority of this interpretation is far from secure. It sits right alongside a radical uncertainty about how the black, diseased, female body and skin is able to represent and hold such absolute difference. The ever-lurking possibility that haunts the extract is that the distances between Gill and the Ugandan woman could have been bridged.

Although I want to focus specifically upon Gill's account in exploring constructions of difference, the conversation between the nurses is important in making sense of the localized dynamics of intercultural care and 'race' thinking, and their interrelationships with wider discourses of cultural competence in nursing. This wider focus will enable us to examine how the nurses are positioned in a complex web of racializing practices and discourses, rather than 'simply' pathologizing Gill as a racist and personalizing her 'failure of care'.

Let us look at how we might explore some of these wider racializing practices and discourses by returning to the point in the extract where Gill raises the possibility – albeit in a very ambivalent way – that she has 'failed' the Ugandan woman: 'I suppose I view that as a failure of care in a way'. In many ways, this is a very personal statement. It points to the emotional content of intercultural care, where the work of care can involve 'emotional labour' (James, 1989) and the management of one's own feelings. In the statement, Gill raises the threatening spectre that she has failed the service user, but her qualification of 'I suppose' works to prevent her from engaging fully with this threat and the blame that accompanies failure. Using the psychoanalytic concept of splitting (see Chapter 2), we can see how Gill might split off her negative anxieties about her own failure of care and project them on to the construction of Ugandan women as guarded and unfathomable. Hence, blame for any failures in care is mediated and shifted from Gill to those categorized as Ugandan women.

This psychoanalytic reading is valuable to our interpretation and in recognizing the contorted emotional dynamics of intercultural care. What is also interesting is that the threat of the possibility of a 'failure' of care is not only avoided by Gill through her reinterpretation of the encounter as one of unbridgeable racialized difference (a reinterpretation that is simultaneously undermined by the nervous laughter that accompanied her awkward qualification of 'I don't know'). The threat of failure, and therefore responsibility and blame, is collaboratively avoided by all the nurses through a series of varied boundaries that they produce between whiteness and Ugandanness, whiteness and professional identity and 'the personal' and the professional.

ACTIVITY 4.4

Re-read Extract 4.3 and try to identify some of the relationships that the nurses produce between:

- whiteness and Ugandanness;
- whiteness and professional identity;
- 'the personal' and 'the professional'.

How do you think these relationships are affected by the specific characteristics of the Ugandan woman in relation to her silence, her AIDS dementia and her closeness to death?

COMMENT

The interrelationships between 'the personal' and a wider context can be seen in how the nurses construct and move between the boundaries of 'the personal' and 'the professional' and, through these movements, make visible particular constructions of gender and 'race'. For example, gender is performed in the dialogue through the binary divisions that the nurses produce between emotionality and rationality. The positioning of the Ugandan woman as closed off and visibly unemotional and uncommunicative (masculine qualities), is an identification that is underpinned by the less obvious and contradictory positioning of the nurses as at once both 'masculine' and 'feminine'. Through the acknowledgement of a possible 'failure' of care the nurses produce themselves as vulnerable and feminine. Masculinity comes into play through their recourse to a model of professional practice based upon the need for practitioners to have a rational mastery of discrete forms of physiological and cultural knowledge, which becomes undermined because successful completion of a training programme is supposed to include acquisition of the skills of such mastery (Gerrish et al., 1996).

These different gendered positions are connected to 'race' through a language of movement in the dialogue. Here, the failure of Gill 'to get alongside' the Ugandan woman, and Roz's questioning of whether her whiteness has 'held me up', reproduce racialized-gendered difference – at certain points in the conversation – as an impermeable boundary between the experiences and understanding of white and black women. This also maps on to a destabilization of their professional identity because, as professionals, they should be able to work with anybody: that is, to transcend social differences. But here their powerful sense of white skin feels as though it is holding them up. The possibility of understanding across racialized boundaries emphasized in the nursing literature is questioned, but is also made more complex by the recognition of the embodied, emotional and organic effects of disease (AIDS dementia).

Further interpretations of the extract come into view if we look at the account in the context of the nursing literature on cultural competence. For instance, we might see Gill's dilemma as being an example of her failure to be competent in the generic skills of 'inter-cultural communicative competence' (see section 3.2). She has not been able to use her cognitive skills to remain open in a situation marked by the threat of difference and non-communication and so has set boundaries to points of identification or connection with the Ugandan woman. Yet, this lack of identification appears to take place despite Gill's references to her knowledge and experience of Ugandan culture, through the other Ugandan women she has nursed. In other words, there is a dissonance within the account between having a rational 'cultural knowledge' and the emotional and cognitive skill of being 'interculturally communicatively competent' and open to difference.

Our examination of the interview extract so far has raised many issues for us to think about in addressing how care can become racialized. It is useful to recap on these issues here where the main points in our discussion have included how:

- notions of biological and cultural difference are central to the construction of embodied racialized difference between Gill and the Ugandan woman;

- the marking of boundaries of difference between Gill and the Ugandan woman involve both emotional and discursive processes;

- the construction of racialized and gendered boundaries are critical to how the nurses produce themselves as white professionals;

- Gill's personal dilemma of intercultural care signifies a gap between individual experiences of care and wider policy and nursing discourses on intercultural care.

All these interpretive insights help us to understand something of the complicated nature of the processes through which racialized relationships of care can be produced and felt in an English hospice ward. Yet, despite the complexity of this psychosocial interpretation, it does not go far enough. It does not enable us to gain insights into how Gill's dilemmas might be connected to other social and cultural spaces. It does not allow us to animate the Ugandan woman so that she is freed from the racializing discourses within

Gill's story, so that we might understand other dimensions of her lived experience of care (I will return to this in section 7.2). And it does not provoke us into examining how we might be implicated in the dynamics within and surrounding Gill's account.

It is in addressing these limitations of interpretation, particularly in making fuller connections between 'the personal' and the social, that I will demonstrate the value of a multi-sited analysis of Gill's account. In order to appreciate how multi-sited approaches are suited to the analysis of accounts of care in multicultural, postcolonial contexts, the next section will examine the relationships between postcoloniality and multi-sited analyses. We will then come back to Gill's account and look at it through a multi-sited lens to see how it can enrich our interpretation.

5   Postcolonialism and multi-sited research

My promotion of multi-sited analyses to understand some of the nuances of racialized experiences and practices in health care organizations comes from a recognition of the ways in which the wider dynamics of postcolonialism are implicated in everyday constructions of 'race' and ethnicity. By postcolonialism, I am referring to complex and ambivalent social, material, epistemological and spatial relationships between the past and present (Ahmed, 2000, p.11), rather than a discrete moment in time. This more complex understanding of postcolonialism, influenced by post-structuralist and cultural theory, engenders a move away from analyses based upon notions of history as linear and social categories and spaces as bounded. In their place we have analyses that draw attention to the relationality of social categories, to the 'entanglements' and 'border crossings [that] are territorial, political, economic, cultural and psychological' (Brah, 1996, p.209).

What this means is that when we look at Britain as a postcolonial space, for example, we need to take into account how different histories of colonialism have shaped and continue to shape contemporary racialized relationships and identities in Britain, not just for those categorized as 'ethnic minorities' but also for those categorized as white, British (Brah, 1996, p.209). Postcolonial analysis thus draws attention to the interconnectedness of social and subjective life across social contexts and time. With this analytic focus we can see the value of methodological approaches that are concerned with mapping and connection as a way of tracing and understanding the interrelationships between identities and social processes.

The recognition of the complexity of relationships between the present and the past and the local and wider contexts is where postcolonialism as a form of interpreting social relationships meets multi-sited approaches. A central strand of this claim is that the questioning and problematizing of key boundaries by postcolonialism – be they spatial, temporal, discursive or interactional – assumes a multi-sited analytic that can track the movement of meanings and practices across boundaries. As Marcus (1998, p.117) has argued in relation to anthropology, but which is also relevant to research in social policy, we can no longer do research with 'the sense that the cultural object of study is fully accessible within a particular site, or without the sense that a site of fieldwork anywhere is integrally and intimately tied to sites of possible fieldwork elsewhere'. So, for example, although my initial analysis of Gill's account has explored constructions of racialized difference and care within a hospice setting, a multi-sited approach to the account would seek to examine how Gill's narrative and predicament relates to and overlaps with social spaces outside of the hospice. In this sense, multi-sited analyses are both deeply embedded in the tight, intimate spaces of a research encounter, and are committed to moving outside it.

Multi-sited approaches are characterized by:

- 'the idea ... that any cultural identity or activity is constructed by multiple agents in varying contexts or places' (Marcus, 1998, p.52) and that our research methods and analyses must be able to represent these flowing and multiple relationships;

- the insistence that researchers examine research narratives for evidence of 'critical consciousness' and 'counter discourses' that are not 'obviously dominant' within accounts but that are vital in suggesting directions for the analysis to move in;

- the need for the researcher to search for relationships of 'complicity' (points of connection and involvement) within the research encounter, in order to explore how the research relationship is orientated to these other social spaces and experiences;

- the responsibility of the researcher to make clear how she or he is bringing other contexts into view through a multi-sited agenda.

In examining what a multi-sited approach might produce for a social policy that is concerned with personal lives, let us return to Gill's account.

6   Reading Gill's account through a multi-sited analysis

In re-examining Gill's account through a multi-sited analysis, I want to begin by looking at the 'points of critical consciousness' (Marcus, 1998, p.53) within it. You will remember that, despite the embodied and emotional boundaries that Gill (and the other nurses) drew between herself and the Ugandan woman, Gill was not certain that these boundaries were 'real'. These fundamental uncertainties about the nature and meanings of 'race' and ethnicity as an uncrossable difference between Gill and the Ugandan woman are the areas of 'critical consciousness' in Gill's racializing discourse. The contradictions of seeking to categorize minoritized service users by their 'race' and ethnicity, alongside models of care and service provision that strive to recognize individual experiences and care needs, are not unique to Gill. Such contradictions saturate local and national policies on 'race' equality and multiculturalism and, as we have seen, they are also evident in professional training and education resources.

What is less obvious, perhaps, is that uncertainties about the usefulness of racial and ethnic categories in engaging with lived experience also mark critical epistemological and political dilemmas in the social sciences. For example, some theorists have argued that concepts of 'race' and ethnicity are so entangled with histories of racism, where individuals and social groups have been categorized and reduced to racial markers such as skin colour, that we should stop using the concepts in our analyses (Gilroy, 2000). This is because the concepts have been seen as being incapable of representing the complexity of human experience, and are also seen as being a critical part of the epistemological process through which racial categorization has been made real. Radhakrishnan (1996, p.81) has captured the analytic ambivalence and the political danger of using racial categories to understand individual lives in his conceptualization of the 'treacherous bind' where '"race" has been the history of an untruth, of an untruth that unfortunately is our history ... The challenge here is to generate, from such a past and a present, a future where race will have been put to rest forever'.

These dilemmas and uncertainties about working with concepts of 'race' and ethnicity in the present, while also wanting to stop the dehumanizing categorization of people by 'race' and ethnicity in the future, mark my own experiences of researching and writing (Gunaratnam, 2003). I highlight them here because they point to an unexpected alignment or 'complicity' between Gill and myself in our research relationship. This complicity relates to how Gill and I negotiate our particular uncertainties and ambivalence in working with racialized categories in our different worlds.

In wanting to trace this complicity in using racial categories, a multi-sited analysis would urge us to recontextualize my research encounter with Gill. To do this, we need to look for the ways in which points of 'critical consciousness' in Gill's account might connect to my own positioning as a social scientist. The work of analysis in this instance is to trace and put together the fragments of discourse that trail between, and are present in, the spaces of Gill's experiences and mine. In many ways the search for these connections jars the lines of analysis, as we move from the site of multicultural hospice service provision to academic concerns with epistemology and the production of knowledge. Although these discontinuities between sites may appear to disrupt and untidy my analysis, they are what characterize multi-sited approaches that aim to chart relationships and affinities between previously unconnected settings. Indeed, it is precisely the strangeness of the connections that are uncovered through our attention to complicity in the research relationship that is the strength of multi-sited approaches and which can lead to richer understandings of what is being examined. In order to make these 'strange' connections I want to turn the ethnographic lens away from the research site and address the academic field of research on 'race' and ethnicity.

7   Other connections, other contexts

As we have seen, the complicity that connects me to Gill is our uncertainty and ambivalence in working with racial and ethnic categories. The epistemological debates about whether and how social scientists should work with the concepts of 'race' and ethnicity are varied and often theoretically dense, seemingly a world away from care practices in the health services. However, as I went back to the academic literature, it became apparent that epistemological concerns about the body and the skin as key signifiers of racialized difference were critical points of overlapping interest for Gill and for me. These points of overlap became clearer in reading Paul Gilroy's (2000) work in which he has examined how scientific discourses originating in the nineteenth century had located 'race' on the surfaces of the body, particularly the skin. Gilroy makes the point that both the physical and the social sciences have played central roles in the development of systems of racial categorization, by generating and legitimizing forms of knowledge in which physical characteristics have come to represent absolute biological, emotional and cultural differences.

7.1   Moving through the skin

You may already have made links between Gilroy's argument and themes in Gill's account, where the 'flat face' of the Ugandan woman is read as a marker of essential difference between Gill and the woman. There are also less obvious links that I would like to make between academic concerns about the continued use of racial and ethnic categories and intercultural hospice care. These questions relate to racialized relationships of the skin and to Gilroy's argument that a significant challenge to our understanding about racialized difference as being visible on the body is being provoked by developments in molecular biology. These scientific developments, that are based upon the reading of microscopic processes deep within the body, Gilroy suggests, have meant that notions of 'race' can no longer be simply constructed as being visible on the surfaces of the body. For Gilroy, developments in microbiology, and the ability of scanning technology such as MRI scanning (nuclear magnetic resonance spectroscopy) to image the body beneath the skin (so that biological abnormalities can be examined), threaten to undermine the nineteenth-century 'perceptual regimes' of racial categorization.

The particular historical power/knowledge relationships in the bio-politics of 'race' addressed by Gilroy have direct relevance to my research encounter with Gill. The group interview extract discussed in section 4 speaks through many of the nuanced racializing codes, caught between the biological and the cultural, that have been identified by Gilroy as serving to dehumanize and oppress racialized others. However, there is also another facet to this kaleidoscope of intermeshing connections that relates to the highly technological world of body imaging depicted by Gilroy. In this world, where technologies are now able to 'see through' the skin, Gilroy suggests that there are new epistemological possibilities for how we think about bodies and racialized bodies in particular. Moreover, this is also a technological world which Gill, the Ugandan woman and I have moved through in our different relationships with the hospice. And it is a world criss-crossed by the uneven contradictions of multicultural and postcolonial relationships. Multi-sited attention to my alignments with Gill thus suggests that the seemingly incongruent site of imaging technology is a point through which we can bring further interpretations to Gill's account.

7.2 Feeling bodies

Body imaging technologies (see, for example, Figure 4.3) are routinely used to examine the spread of disease (including cerebral infection relating to AIDS) within the body. However, they are much more than technologies that constitute new ways of understanding, observing and coding the body. As Quayson and Goldberg (2002) have observed, technological advances always bring with them certain ontological experiences of technology. In making connections between Gill's account and my own positioning I want to explore how attention to these ontological experiences can bring new insights and questions to our reading of Gill's narrative.

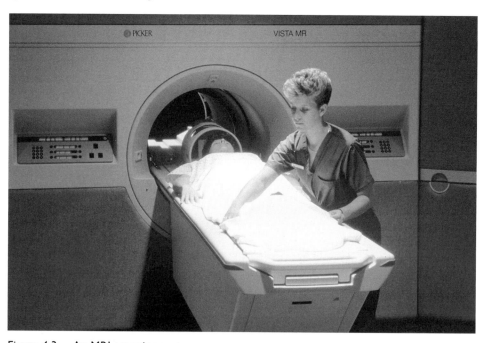

Figure 4.3   An MRI scanning system

Perhaps somewhat obviously, my identification of imaging technologies as a strand of connection between myself and Gill, led me to narratives from other hospice service users in my research and to accounts of having an MRI scan. One vivid account came from 'Hilda' (a pseudonym), a black Jamaican woman with cancer who had been a hospital 'domestic' (someone who cleans and can be involved in the serving of food) before her illness. In our interviews, Hilda had talked spontaneously about the 'frightening scenery' and trauma of her first experience of being scanned. Indeed, many people can find the personal experience of body imaging terrifying, reporting feelings of fear and claustrophobia (McIsaac et al., 1998), with some people experiencing panic attacks, that can often lead to the termination of a scan (see MacKenzie et al., 1995).

Hilda described the MRI scanner as 'like a sepulchre' into which she was taken by the push of a button and where she had to lie perfectly still, listening to the loud 'knocking' sounds of the machine while 'praying to the lord to help me come out'. Rationalizing the experience in terms of 'needing to find out what was going on' inside her body, and spiritualizing her mode of enduring the scan, Hilda's account of an MRI scan was underwritten by a series of embodied–emotional dynamics relating to the negotiation of space, isolation, fear, immobilization, discipline, powerlessness and containment.

These themes in Hilda's description of being scanned, as part of a process that would enable diagnosis and treatment – that might make her 'better' – resonated further with emotional themes in her story of migration to England in the 1950s. Despite conditions being 'very rough' in relation to overt racism, exclusion from housing, and poverty, Hilda was clear that 'you can't go back' and need to 'press along, hoping that better days will come'. Here is a quote from my interview with Hilda, when she talked about her 'perseverance' in the face of very overt forms of racism:

> Well you have to press through. You're in the country and you have your families back home, you can't go back 'cause you come, you have to try and do something that let me press along. Yeah, you press along, hoping that better days will come. Perseverance and because of perseverance, here I am. Yes.

In considering associations between Hilda's accounts of migration and settlement and her experiences of an MRI scan, I want to focus upon emotional and socio-economic connections. For me, there is a real sense in which Hilda's ability to 'benefit' from body imaging technology is both a connective and a discrepant link in a much wider emotional and socio-economic chain of postcolonial relationships that also connects Hilda to the Ugandan woman in Gill's account.

In terms of the emotional, we can see from Hilda's story of her period of early settlement in England that there are points of resonance between her experiences of quiet 'perseverance' and the emotional and bodily 'patience' demanded in medical care. Wider research has suggested that medical and nursing practices can be particularly 'muting' for minoritized women, where women's wider social and cultural experiences can be denied or misinterpreted (Bowler, 1993; Gunaratnam, 2004). Questions of both the emotional dimensions of care and how specific philosophies of care (such as holistic nursing) impact upon different service users are important in understanding these processes of silencing and provide a further context for interpreting Gill's account.

Bowler (1993), for example, in her ethnographic study of users of maternity services from South-Asian backgrounds in the South of England, found that the women were often categorized as 'bad patients' and were 'unpopular' among the white nursing staff. A significant issue in Bowler's study was the emotional impact upon the nurses where women could not communicate effectively with them in English. Bowler writes that:

> A theme running through the data ... is the role of communication difficulties which may be seen as a major factor in negative typification of Asian women. Because of these problems it can be more difficult and time consuming for midwives to care for them. Menzies (1960) leads us to expect that patients who cause a high level of anxiety or who cause staff to feel ineffective or angry ... may become negatively typified.
>
> Accepting a rigid stereotyped view of Asian women may act as a defence against the anxiety generated in staff who cannot communicate with them. Stereotyping can allow staff to make assumptions about the care women need (or deserve).
>
> (Bowler, 1993, pp.172–3)

In relation to the Ugandan woman in Gill's account, the question of the woman's silence and lack of communication with the nurses is extremely complicated when taking into consideration her AIDS dementia. But, what we cannot ignore is that the nurses failed to locate the woman's silence within a broader social context. This situating of the woman's silence may have enabled the nurses to recognize the unconscious emotional dynamics of intercultural care (how their own anxieties about racialized difference might affect their care and have silencing effects upon service users). It might also have helped them to consider the threatening nature of the surveillance aspects of holistic care (that enquires into emotional and social circumstances) for minoritized women and people with AIDS. For example, research commissioned by the Department of Health on 'Black African Communities' living in England (Elam and Chinouya, 2000) has suggested that fear of stigmatization because of HIV/AIDS can be silencing for many individuals.

In my hospice research, my tape-recorded interview with James, a Kenyan man with AIDS, was marked by purposeful silences and the non-naming of AIDS. These presented particular difficulties for how James was able to tell his life story and for our interaction within the interview (see Gunaratnam, 2003). Despite his strong identifications of being 'a proud Kenyan' and his involvement in African community groups, James's secrecy about his AIDS had isolated him from his family and community networks, and there were strong tensions in his account between being a 'proud Kenyan' and 'living with AIDS'. AIDS in this sense is a disease that not only involves a brutal assault upon the body, it is also a disease that carries social and moral meanings (Lather and Smithies, 1997) that can assault communication, relationships and identifications.

ACTIVITY 4.5

The writing in Extract 4.4 was evoked by my interview with James. When you are reading it think about the personal interrelationships between you, me and James that are produced through the act of reading. Consider the ideas of Boler, a social theorist, about reading as an act of testimony (a responsibility to tell) and her suggestion that readers should ask themselves 'what crisis of truth does this text speak to, and what mass of contradictions and struggles do I become as a result?' (Boler, 1997, p.270).

Extract 4.4   Testify

He walked with slow, graceful steps into the small side-room of the hospice ward, his eyes focussed on the tape recorder. As he talked, and stopped himself from talking, he passed me his life, slowly, under the table, when no one was looking. The silences and gaps in his story said 'Here it is. The unimaginable. The unspeakable. Do something with it.' He gave me few facts. No names. No places. No faces. Travelling light, he set me on my way with the gentlest of hand-shakes.

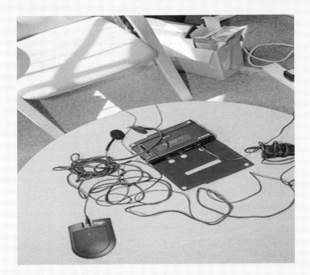

Figure 4.4

Twenty-two million people dead so far. Thirty-six million people infected. One 40 year-old man alone, facing me, in this tiny room with his deadly secret. Cut off from family and friends, with a few more weeks to live. So frightened, so ashamed he can't even name the disease out loud.

Drawn in quickly by the fear, our conversation becomes encoded. We talk about his 'illness'. 'The disease'. 'The terminal condition'. This shared, lacy language, mocks the tape-recorder. My assurances of confidentiality and anonymity become meaningless. Nothing is ever really private. We both know that. So he plays shame at its own game, using silence to unhinge distinctions between the public and private, safety and danger, openness and secrecy. And so, his muted story says it all, loud and clear, reproducing in full technicolour the meanings of dis-ease in his life.

And with fear breathing down his neck, he has somehow walked into this room and taken one last chance to tell his story. He has taken a chance not only with me, but with you too. To bear witness, he does not need you to come close, to enter his life through the details, and in consuming him, forget who you are. Stay where you are on that side of the table. On that side of the page. Don't let your hand move towards him, when it becomes too much. Don't feel guilty. When rage, disbelief and confusion tear you apart, move into the chasm that separates you. And wonder about yourself.

What emerges when I engage with these other contexts of my research through a multi-sited analysis is how silence from service users in situations of intercultural care can be highly problematic for nurses (on this see, for example, Davidhizar and Newman Giger, 1994), particularly where there is a need to engage with emotional and social experiences. Carl May (1992) has suggested in relation to holistic 'new nursing' practices, that silence can constitute significant forms of resistance and agency for service users:

> the subjectification of patients or clients implies a new locus of power for them. Unlike the 'truth' of the disordered body, visible through examination or biochemistry, the truth of the subject cannot be exposed without the explicit permission of the subject concerned. It cannot be exposed or fixed without positive action on the part of the patient, who may lie or remain silent in the face of such enquiry. The question 'do you want to talk' offers the possibility of answering 'no'.
>
> (May, 1992, p.600)

As you will have noticed, the mapping of experiences of body scanning as a connective thread between racializing discourses, care practices and embodied experience through my multi-sited analysis deepens our interpretation of Gill's account and enables further readings of the silence of the Ugandan woman. Although my interpretations are necessarily limited in the sense that we are not able to hear the Ugandan woman's story, the analysis suggests the implausibility of reading her silence through her Ugandanness and the woman becomes more than an indecipherable 'flat face'.

My reinterpretation of Gill's account so far, using a multi-sited analysis, has been developed by moving through three very different social spaces: the epistemological, the local professional/institutional and the technological, pulling several wider social and emotional contexts into our frame of interpretation. These contexts have included:

- how epistemological tensions in Gill's account about the validity of 'race' as a concept in interpreting human behaviour resonate with academic debates;

- my own embodied entanglements in the epistemological and political debates about racial and ethnic categories within the social sciences and the connections between these debates and my hospice research, through the technology of scanning;

- the juxtapositioning of the epistemological dimensions of the technology (Gilroy's (2000) suggestion that body imaging technology might challenge racial thinking) alongside an account from Hilda, a hospice service user, of the experience of being scanned;

- the ambiguities of silence within a context of racialized social relationships and AIDS oppression.

These very different contexts have made my analysis of Gill's account complicated in terms of interpretation and they have also pointed to some of the postcolonial and material contradictions of multicultural health care. It is a concern with exploring these contradictions further that directs my multi-sited analysis back to Gill.

8   Postcolonial collisions

As a white British hospice nurse, Gill is another link in these postcolonial dynamics, where her ontological experiences of scanning technology are both diffuse and subtle. Gill will almost certainly have had some generalized familiarity with developments in molecular biology in diagnostic testing and screening, and imaging technologies and scanning. She will sometimes have counselled service users before and after different tests. She would have helped to prepare some of them about what to expect when their bodies are scanned, and it is likely that she would have accompanied some hospice service users to imaging appointments. Gill is someone who, through a wide range of experiences of nursing, 'knows' about the biological meaninglessness of 'race' in the deep structures of the body and in matters of death and dying.

Despite this 'knowledge', the idea of 'race' coded and etched into the skin, body and the mind of the Ugandan woman is overwhelming in the account of Gill's dilemma of caring for her. This is a particularly acute contradiction when we consider the notions of a common humanity embedded in the Christian-based ethos of hospice care and often given an added impetus through therapeutic discourses of 'holistic care'. It gives us an inkling of the power and tenacity of racial thinking, and also speaks to its complexity and contradictions. It is here that the everyday worlds of interracial encounters in multicultural hospice wards, postcolonial bio-politics and the worlds of research on 'race' and ethnicity collide and are complicit, constructing uncomfortable affinities and alignments in very different relationships of care.

As far as Gill's account reflects and constructs dominant discourses of 'race', we can see that the 'oppositional space' (Marcus, 1998) within this discourse – that is, what threatens to unravel it – lies not simply in the tensions spotlighted between 'race' and 'humanness' but with whether to use racial categories or to abandon them. As I have pointed out earlier, these tensions run across the academic study of 'race' and ethnicity, and can be witnessed in my own experiences of researching and writing about 'race' and ethnicity. What is perhaps more challenging for us to understand is that, while there are real differences between the social positions that Gill and I occupy, the questions that we both pursue about the meanings and the relevance of racial and ethnic categories in the everyday are broadly similar.

Such uncomfortable commonalities bring us to the political ambivalence of complicity. The ambivalence that I am referring to relates to more than epistemological dilemmas in using racial and ethnic categories. It is also played out across the socio-economic discrepancies of multicultural health care and can be witnessed in how Gill's story of her encounters with the Ugandan woman is located within particular social and material contexts. At a fundamental level, there are stark disparities in health care and the treatment of HIV/AIDS between those in the North/West and those in developing countries. For example, the patents and prices of drugs used in the treatment and management of HIV and AIDS-related conditions are controlled by multinational drug companies and trade protection legislation, resulting in many drugs being too expensive for developing countries to buy (see Figures 4.5 and 4.6). As a result of these dynamics in the international pharmaceutical markets, that are themselves a part of wider global economic disparities, vast inequalities exist in the treatment of HIV and AIDS, and therefore also in mortality rates from the disease, between, for example, sub-Saharan Africa and Britain (*New Internationalist*, June 2002, pp.18–19).

Figure 4.5   Demonstrators protest against drug trade protection legislation

The unnamed woman, reduced in Gill's account to her ethnicity, gender and her AIDS, left this world no doubt with the best (physical) pain and symptom

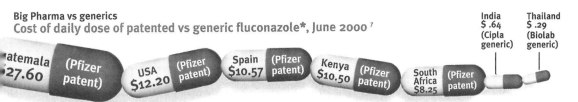

Big Pharma vs generics
Cost of daily dose of patented vs generic fluconazole*, June 2000 [7]

Guatemala $27.60 (Pfizer patent)   USA $12.20 (Pfizer patent)   Spain $10.57 (Pfizer patent)   Kenya $10.50 (Pfizer patent)   South Africa $8.25 (Pfizer patent)   India $ .64 (Cipla generic)   Thailand $ .29 (Biolab generic)

*Fluconazole (its generic name is diflucan) is an anti-fungal drug commonly used
against oral thrush and cryptococcal meningitis, both of which attack people with HIV.

Figure 4.6   Postcolonial inequalities in health care: trade protection makes some drugs unaffordable for developing countries

control, pioneered by technological and pharmaceutical innovations in Northern/Western palliative care, and within a context of service provision struggling to recognize cultural difference as a part of wider British public-sector commitments to multicultural service provision. The tensions between local multicultural commitments and broader postcolonial relationships can be witnessed in the contradictions that surround, and are embedded in, Gill's account.

The Ugandan woman's gendered and racialized otherness, at a time when concerns about cultural sensitivity in hospice care were clearly troubling the hospice movement and hospice professionals (in which my research is also implicated), afforded the woman some of the 'special privileges' that are now a routine part of multicultural service developments. For example, later in the group interview Gill talked about how she had contacted a local black community group that had previously offered support to the woman in the community. On Gill's initiative, a representative from the group had visited the woman at the hospice, although Gill suggested that the woman still 'kept a distance' from the visitor. It is also highly likely that Gill would have made efforts to ensure the availability of 'Ugandan food' for the woman, as she had talked about the importance of the provision of 'ethnic' food options to minoritized service users at other points in the group interview when talking about a Ugandan service user (see Gunaratnam, 2001).

Such effects of racial thinking may have produced specific beneficial/benefactory outcomes for the Ugandan woman (outcomes that she herself may have been aware of), within particular sites and relationships of global bio-politics and of localized, anxious multicultural service provision. But they too become more uncertain when the 'evil' effects of concepts of 'race', that Gilroy has addressed, are attended to. Gill's description of her failure to 'get alongside' the Ugandan woman because of 'cultural differences' suggests that the woman left this world tended to, but also imprisoned and isolated by the bio-political effects of 'race' in an English hospice ward. It is more than likely that the woman's physical care needs were addressed, and that she received better pain control and symptom management than she would have received in Uganda. However, a question mark hangs over the care that she received for her emotional needs and experiences and this lack is a fundamental issue with which we are confronted in Gill's account and through our attention to relationships of complicity.

For me, the particular analytic insights that multi-sited forms of interpretation offer come with this attention to complicity. With regard to my research relationship with Gill, we can see how the search for moments of shared orientation has been pivotal to the analysis and has not allowed me to distance myself from Gill by categorizing her narrative as racist. Attention to complicity pushed me to try to piece together how in the co-production of Gill's account there were points of alignment in the apparent distances between us that were connected to different sites of the research setting and to epistemological dilemmas about the use of racial categories. This is what directed the analysis to the academic debates, and through these debates brought me to the epistemological and experiential dimensions of medical technology, to postcolonial inequalities and to the contradictions of multicultural service provision.

In bringing this roving analysis to a close I want to raise the question of ethics more explicitly through the triangular relationship between Gill, me and you, the reader. A significant challenge for us is how to engage with Gill's account in ways that testify to her location within complicated local and global bio-political relationships and at the same time treat the account of her experiences of intercultural care with some degree of sympathy (on this see, for example, Marcus, 1998, p.123). Care as an analytic practice in this context raises the fundamental question of how, when we make connections between 'the personal' and the social, we might use multi-sited analysis to reflect upon and confront the meanings of our own positioning within the complex power relationships that we have excavated.

9 Conclusion

In this chapter, I have drawn upon ideas about 'multi-sited' research, developed in the field of ethnography, to examine how we might use qualitative research and analysis to think in new ways about the interrelationships between 'the personal' and the social. What I hope to have demonstrated through my multi-sited analysis of Gill's account is how 'the personal' can be used to produce knowledge about contexts and experiences that are often beyond our immediate and/or imaginable frames of reference.

The analytic movements to and fro between my research encounter with Gill and other local and wider contexts – enabled through attention to relationships of complicity – have suggested that the research encounter is connected to two main sites. One grapples with the discrepancies and inadequacies of racial and ethnic categories that are no longer 'good to think with' but which have yet to be replaced (Hall, 1996). The other is located within the emotional and socio-economic contradictions of multicultural care in a global arena of continuing, and often stark, postcolonial inequalities. The recognition of these diverse links suggests new sites of dialogue within social policy about the meanings, nature and extents of what we see as 'care' in racialized contexts. What I also want to suggest is that, in recognizing very different individuals as being concerned and connected to broader contexts, multi-sited analysis can use 'the personal' to bring about a different way of engaging with questions of social justice and inequality.

In my interpretation this form of engagement involves using the interpersonal that is always generated through research and the act of reading to initiate dialogue and exchange between apparently different worlds of experience. It is a commitment to this version of 'the personal', as a domain that implicates researchers and readers as much as research participants, professionals and service users, and a domain that is always already connected to 'great and little events happening elsewhere' (Marcus, 1998, p.118) that can transform our approaches to lived experiences of racialized care.

Further resources

Two main topics are discussed in this chapter: 'race' and professional care in the health services, and social research methods and 'race'. If you would like to do some further reading around 'race' and care, a good starting-point would be Ahmad's edited collection *'Race' and Health in Contemporary Britain* (1993) which provides a conceptual overview together with a broad-ranging discussion of health policy and practice from researchers and those working in the health services. Culley and Dyson's *Ethnicity and Nursing Practice* (2001), featuring the work of nurses and nurse educators, uses sociological theories to understand the inter-relationships between 'race', ethnicity and nursing practice. Edited collections by Stanfield and Dennis (*'Race' and Ethnicity in Research Methods*, 1993) and by Winddance Twine and Warren (*Racing Research, Researching Race*, 2000) combine historical and conceptual analyses with reflexive accounts of methodological practice and dilemmas in fieldwork from the USA. Yasmin Gunaratnam's *Researching 'Race' and Ethnicity* (2003) applies postcolonial theory to research and uses in-depth analyses of research interactions in an English hospice. Marcus's *Ethnography Through Thick and Thin* (1998) provides a detailed, provocative but sometimes dense discussion of multi-sited research practices.

AIDS Epidemic Update, UNAIDS, December 2001: www.unaids.org (accessed on 11 January 2004).

References

Ahmad, W. (ed.) (1993) *Race and Health in Contemporary Britain*, Buckingham, Open University Press.

Ahmed, S. (2000) *Strange Encounters, Embodied Others in Post-Coloniality*, London, Routledge.

Alexander, Z. (1999) *Study of Black, Asian and Ethnic Minority Issues*, London, Department of Health.

Boler, M. (1997) 'The risks of empathy: interrogating multiculturalism's gaze', *Cultural Studies*, vol.11, no.2, pp.253–73.

Bowler, I. (1993) 'They're not the same as us: midwives' stereotypes of South Asian descent maternity patients', *Sociology of Health and Illness*, vol.15, no.2, pp.157–78.

Brah, A. (1996) *Cartographies of Diaspora: Contesting Identities*, London, Routledge.

Brenner, P. (1997) 'Issues of access in a diverse society', *The Hospice Journal*, vol.12, no.2, pp.9–16.

Clark, D. (1993) *Partners in Care? Hospices and Health Authorities*, Aldershot, Avebury.

Culley, L. and Dyson, S. (eds) (2001) *Ethnicity and Nursing Practice*, London, Palgrave.

Davidhizar, R. and Newman Giger, J. (1994) 'When your patient is silent', *Journal of Advanced Nursing*, vol.20, no.3, pp.703–6.

Department of Health (2000) *The Vital Connection: An Equalities Framework for the NHS*, London, Department of Health Publications.

Elam, G. and Chinouya, M. (2000) *Feasibility Study for Health Surveys Among Black African Populations Living in the UK: Stage 2 – Diversity Among Black African Communities*, London, National Centre for Social Research.

English National Board for Nursing, Midwifery and Health Visiting (1990) *Regulations and Guidelines for the Approval of Institutions and Courses*, London, English National Board for Nursing, Midwifery and Health Visiting.

Firth, S. (2001) *Wider Horizons: Care of the Dying in a Multicultural Society*, London, National Council for Hospice and Specialist Palliative Care Services.

Gerrish, K., Husband, C. and Mackenzie, J. (1996) *Nursing for a Multi-Ethnic Society*, Buckingham, Open University Press.

Gilroy, P. (2000) *Nations, Cultures and the Allure of Race: Between Camps*, London, Allen Lane.

Green, J. (1991) *Death with Dignity: Meeting the Spiritual Needs of Patients in a Multi-Cultural Society*, A *Nursing Times* Publication, London, Macmillan Magazines.

Green, J. (1992) *Death with Dignity: Meeting the Spiritual Needs of Patients in a Multi-Cultural Society*, vol.2, London, Macmillan Magazines.

Gunaratnam, Y. (1997) 'Culture is not enough: a critique of multi-culturalism in palliative care' in Field, D., Hockey, J. and Small, N. (eds) *Death, Gender and Ethnicity*, London, Routledge.

Gunaratnam, Y. (2001) 'Eating into multi-culturalism: hospice staff and service users talk food, "race", ethnicity and identities', *Critical Social Policy*, vol.21, no.3, pp.287–310.

Gunaratnam, Y. (2003) *Researching 'Race' and Ethnicity: Methods, Knowledge, Power*, London, Sage Publications.

Gunaratnam, Y. (2004) 'Bucking and kicking': "race", gender and embodied resistance in health care' in Apitzsch, U., Bornat, J. and Chamberlayne, P. (eds) *Biographical Methods and Professional Practice: An International Perspective*, Bristol, The Policy Press.

Gunaratnam, Y. and Lewis, G. (2001) 'Racializing emotional labour and emotionalizing racialized labour: anger, fear and shame in social welfare', *Journal of Social Work Practice*, vol.15, no.2, pp.131–48.

Hall, S. (1996) 'Introduction: who needs identity?' in Hall, S. and du Gay, P. (eds) *Questions of Cultural Identity*, London, Sage Publications.

Hill, D. and Penso, D. (1995) *Opening Doors: Improving Access to Hospice and Specialist Care Services by Members of Black and Ethnic Minority Communities*, London, National Council of Hospice and Specialist Palliative Care Services.

Hollway, W. and Jefferson, T. (2000) *Doing Qualitative Research Differently: Free Association, Narrative and the Interview Method*, London, Sage Publications.

Hospice Information (2002) *Directory 2002: Hospice and Palliative Care Service in the United Kingdom and the Republic of Ireland*, London, Hospice Information.

James, N. (1989) 'Emotional labour: skill and work in the social regulation of feelings', *Sociological Review*, vol.37, pp.15–47.

James, N. and Field, D. (1992) 'The routinization of hospice: charisma and bureaucratization', *Social Science and Medicine,* vol.34, no.12, pp.1362–75.

Khan, U. (2001) *Equality Standards in Health and Social Care: A Scoping Study*, London, Department of Health, Equality Strategy Unit.

Kim, Y.Y. (1989) 'Explaining interethnic conflict' in Gittler, J. (ed.) *The Annual Review of Conflict Knowledge and Conflict Resolution*, New York, Garland.

Kim, Y.Y. (1992) 'Intercultural communication competence: a systems-theoretic view' in Gudykunst, W.B. and Kim, Y.Y. (eds) *Readings on Communication with Strangers*, New York, McGraw-Hill.

Lather, P. and Smithies, C. (1997) *Troubling the Angels: Women Living with HIV/AIDS*, Boulder, CO, Westview Press.

Lewis, G. (1998) 'Welfare and the social construction of "race"' in Saraga, E. (ed.) *Embodying the Social: Constructions of Difference*, London, Routledge in association with The Open University.

MacKenzie, R., Sims, C., Owens, R.G. and Dixon, A.K. (1995) 'Patients' perceptions of magnetic resonance imaging', *Clinical Radiology,* vol.50, no.3, pp.137–43.

Marcus, G.E. (1998) *Ethnography Through Thick and Thin*, Princeton, NJ, Princeton University Press.

May, C. (1992) 'Individual care: power and subjectivity in therapeutic relationships', *Sociology*, vol.26, pp.589–602.

McIsaac, H.K., Thordarson, D.S., Shafran, R., Rachman, S. and Poole, G. (1998) 'Claustrophobia and the magnetic resonance imaging procedure', *Journal of Behavioural Medicine*, vol.21, no.3, pp.255–68.

Menzies, L. (1960) 'A case study in the functioning of social systems as a defence against anxiety: a report on a study of the nursing service of a general hospital', *Human Relations*, vol.13, pp.19–21.

Papadopoulos, I., Tilki, M. and Taylor, G. (1998) *Transcultural Care: A Guide for Health Care Professionals,* Wiltshire, Quay Books.

Quayson, A. and Goldberg, D. (2002) 'Introduction: scale and sensibility' in Goldberg, D. and Quayson, A. (eds) *Relocating Postcolonialism*, Oxford, Blackwell.

Radhakrishnan, R. (1996) *Diasporic Mediations Between Home and Location*, Minneapolis, MN, University of Minnesota Press.

Sielbold, C. (1992) *The Hospice Movement: Easing Death's Pains*, New York, Twyne.

Skeggs, B. (2001) 'Feminist ethnography' in Atkinson, P., Coffey, A., Delamont, S., Loftland, J. and Loftland, L. (eds) *Handbook of Ethnography*, London, Sage Publications.

Stanfield, J. and Dennis, R. (eds) (1993) *'Race' and Ethnicity in Research Methods*, Newbury Park, CA, Sage Publications.

Winddance Twine, F. and Warren, J. (eds) (2000) *Racing Research, Researching Race*, New York, New York University Press.

CHAPTER 5

Care: Meanings, Identities and Morality

by Janet Fink

Contents

1   Introduction

In this book we have examined a number of different ideas, debates and concerns in our exploration of the ways in which care can be understood as a central feature in the mutual constitution of personal lives and social policy.

Aims   Using the lens of care to examine this process of mutual constitution, the aims of the book have been:

- To illustrate that care relations, practices and activities occur in a range of spaces and places, and that these varying locations inflect the links between care, personal lives and social policy in different ways.

- To show that people make sense of ideas about care in very different ways, not least because of the trajectories of their own personal lives and the way these have been influenced by:

    (i) their social location, in terms of gender, age, dis/ability, 'race', class, sexuality and marital status;

    (ii) the interventions of welfare practitioners and policy discourses.

- To argue that it is not only ideas and discourses about care, but also the material and historical contexts in which care takes place, that influence personal lives, welfare practice and policy-making.

- To highlight that issues of power, conflict and control are central to understanding how care relations impact upon our personal lives and attract policy interventions.

- To demonstrate that different theoretical perspectives highlight particular aspects of care relations, and thus bring into view the multiple connections between social policy and personal lives.

Although the above have been identified as separate points, they are nevertheless closely intertwined and there are many points of dynamic intersection between them. This final chapter will, therefore, point to some of the common themes that run through these intersections, and consider how they throw further light on the relationship between personal lives, the practices of welfare professionals and social policy. We have chosen to focus upon the themes of meanings, identities and morality but, of course, your reading of the chapters may have identified other themes in the topics that have been discussed. For instance, you may have noted the attention paid to the significance of social divisions, to the importance of a historical approach and of identifying historical contexts, or to the value that is placed on qualitative research evidence and, in particular, interviews and their analysis. Each of these will emerge in the sections that follow and demonstrate the ways in which different themes criss-cross the course materials.

2   Meanings

This book has paid particular attention to the meanings that are related to care and, equally, to the ambiguities, contradictions and complexities in those meanings. Such an emphasis has illustrated that the issue of care, in both the past and the present, needs careful interrogation and that we must move beyond everyday assumptions about who provides care, who is in need of care and where care takes place in order to begin unpacking its complexities. Overall, the chapters have illustrated how care can mean activities, practices and relationships and that, in all these 'meanings', it can be a site of contestation, not only in policy-making but also in our personal lives. Moreover, the different foci of the chapters serve to demonstrate the many sites where care relations take place and, thereby, problematize normative beliefs that care is located in the home and that it is primarily undertaken, unpaid, by female relatives or friends. In this we have sought to challenge the ways in which, as David Morgan (1996, p.99) has pointed out, '[t]he terms "care" and "family" are frequently and effortlessly bracketed together in social science analysis as well as in ideological or policy statements'.

Our interrogation of care has emphasized the ways in which care straddles and unsettles the boundaries between paid and unpaid employment, work and home, rationality and emotion, masculine and feminine. In particular, we have argued that care is a relational process since it is both given and received, and that it is by paying attention to this interactive factor that we can throw light on what ideas shape and inform care relations. This relational and dynamic process by which care relations are produced brings important insights to our exploration of the connections that care has to our personal lives and to the making of social policy.

The authors have each explored different dimensions of care and, in so doing, foregrounded how a concern with particular theoretical approaches, social divisions and spaces/places of care inform and shape the focus, interests and analytical concerns of research into care. While the meanings afforded to care may thus differ across the chapters, together they demonstrate the presence of a 'continuum of care' (Twigg, 2000, p.2), which can range from love, nurture and personal attention through to abuse and neglect. At all stages of this continuum, issues of power, conflict and control emerge and shape the relationship between those giving and those receiving care. We start with Chapter 3 by Barry Goldson, which engages consistently with these issues although, as we will demonstrate, they are present throughout the book as a whole.

In Chapter 3, the interrogation of meanings of care is driven by Goldson's emphasis on how the implementation of laws, policies and practices to 'care' for children also subject them to the power and control of adults and the state. He rejects, therefore, oversimplified and benign conceptualizations of care (see Chapter 3, section 1). His discussion of the development of institutions for children whose childhoods were perceived to be disadvantaged, at risk, or out of control, illustrates very clearly the unstable boundary between 'doing for' (caring) and 'doing to' (controlling). We can see that his emphasis on poverty, disadvantage and exclusion is informed by the neo-Marxist lens through which he analyses the lives of children in specific types of locked institutions. But, he also draws upon the tools of social constructionism to interrogate the meanings of childhood(s) and the constitution of children as 'victims' or 'threats'. Using these two theoretical approaches, he argues that categorizing children as 'victims' or 'threats' opens up their personal lives and those of their families to scrutiny and intervention by welfare/justice agencies and professionals and, in turn, shapes and regulates those lives because of their failure to meet normative standards. He queries the legitimacy of this intervention by arguing that the children who are targeted are almost always from ' … a skewed population drawn from the most disadvantaged sections of society where class, "race" and gender intersect and overlap in complex formations' (Chapter 3, section 5). It is the personal lives of such children that are subjected to the caring *and* controlling functions of the law, social policy and welfare practices. Chapter 3 illustrates the ways in which the administration of care by the state and its delivery by welfare/justice professionals to particular constituencies of children is a complex process. In this context care cannot be understood as simply meaning nurture, treatment or support, since it also represents control, punishment and regulation. As Goldson argues, for vulnerable children – whether defined as 'victims' or 'threats' – such contradictory meanings and how they are played out in the day-to-day regimes of institutions can have profound effects on the trajectories of their personal lives.

Chapter 4 by Yasmin Gunaratnam is also concerned with the meanings of care in institutional settings but, in this case, within the health services and, in particular, hospices. However, her purpose in exploring care is to inform not only professional practice but also analytic practice. This approach reveals two other strands to the meanings of care. First, Gunaratnam is determined to produce a 'caring' analysis. By this she means not just examining the complexities of both the meanings of 'race' and ethnicity and the processes by which they are constituted in contemporary Britain, but also ensuring that the affinities between the researcher and the research participant 'are recognized and cared about' (Chapter 4, section 2.2). She explains this involvement as 'complicity', and argues that it is significant because it foregrounds the connections between 'the personal' and the social in the research relationship.

Second, Gunaratnam considers how care becomes racialized and the effects of this upon the personal lives of welfare professionals and service users alike. Where Goldson was concerned with power in the context of the overlapping boundaries of care and control, Gunaratnam uses a postcolonial perspective to explore how questions of power are played out in care relations. She argues, therefore, that analysis of the intersections of care, 'race' and ethnicity means that attention must be given to the relationships of power between the past and the present, the local and the global. As one way of illustrating this, she considers how approaches to the education and training needs of professionals produce meanings of racialized care which, in turn, construct the personal lives of service users of different minoritized groups in particular ways.

The result, she argues, is that the rhetoric of cultural competence and 'culturalist' approaches '... can serve to define and reduce needs and experiences primarily to 'race', ethnicity and/or religion, thereby failing to engage with how other forms of social difference (such as gender, class and age) and unique biographical differences can affect the personal meanings of 'race' and ethnicity' (see Chapter 4, section 3.2). The special significance afforded to 'cultural differences' in social policy and welfare practice for the delivery of effective and appropriate care is shown to be deeply problematic. For example, we see how welfare professionals use such differences to constitute minoritized service users as 'other', thereby often reinforcing – rather than questioning or challenging – racializing practices and discourses of care. The racialized meanings of care in the health services are thus shown to have connections to the personal lives of the hospice nurses and the service users as well as to academic debates, policy initiatives and postcolonial inequalities. However, these meanings are never stable and are subject to contestation and negotiation as welfare professionals try to make sense (rationally and emotionally) of the gaps between policy initiatives and their own practices and experiences.

The contested meanings of care, and the different forms of power and control contained within them, are equally evident in Katherine Holden's discussion in Chapter 2 of single women and their care activities in inter-war Britain. Using feminism as one of her analytic lenses, Holden explores the ways in which definitions of care include both paid and unpaid work, and the difficulties that this duality created for unmarried women during the 1920s and 1930s. What emerges are how gendered notions about the meanings of care impacted upon the lives of women who were undertaking care and service work – paid and unpaid – in both the 'public' and 'private' spheres. In this, policy assumptions that women would leave paid employment on marriage to be supported financially by their husbands in order to perform their 'natural' caring roles of wife and mother were crucial. Such assumptions that, on the one hand, women would marry and, on the other, that they would be financially dependent upon their husbands, were used to justify the lower wages and unemployment benefits paid to women. Such inequalities were detrimental to the personal lives of all women, but particularly so for single women who were often expected by the state to be financially independent, to contribute financially to the support of their parents and to provide unpaid care to family members if needed.

The difficulties that single women experienced in negotiating the different expectations that they would take up roles as paid carers in the emerging sphere of welfare services and as unpaid carers in the domestic sphere, were magnified by the contradictory representations of them in wider social and cultural contexts. Such representations ranged from the heroic and dutiful to the interfering and frustrated, and thus illustrate some of the ambivalence with which – in the past and today – we regard our real and imagined need for care and the nature of its delivery. As Holden points out, 'the difficulty many of us have in making clear boundaries between paid and unpaid caring work is still a live issue' (Chapter 2, section 4). Such boundaries have become increasingly hard to maintain as the trajectories of our personal lives shift and adapt to changing demographic, social and economic trends. Yet, at the same time, the slippery and contested meanings of care continue to have profound significance for our social relations with others and our sense of self.

3 Identities

Each of the preceding chapters has looked, to greater and lesser degrees, at how relationships of care – in all their different manifestations – shape and inform a sense of self in the people who give and receive care. However, defining oneself or being defined as a 'carer' is shown to be a complex process that:

1 can be resisted, negotiated or accepted as a valid and valuable role;

2 changes over the life course;

3 shifts depending on the circumstances of identity and subjectivity formation.

In addition, being designated a carer does not always mean that individuals are able to 'do' care or 'be' caring, as the following quotation from *Mother Can You Hear Me?*, a novel by Margaret Forster, illustrates:

> They needed a bedpan and they did not have one. The local shops would not have one. She would have to leave Sadie [her daughter] in charge and go out in search of one. She would have to learn to do the necessary things like putting Mother on a bedpan – things that other people did so sensibly in a sensible matter-of-fact way but from which she shrank. No good muttering about getting a nurse as Ben [her husband] had muttered – nurses could not be so easily got, and even if found and employed they were in this situation a coward's way out.
>
> (Forster, 1981, pp.203–4)

Being designated a carer can be demanding and alien. But, being constituted as needing or deserving care by welfare practitioners, family or friends can be an equally difficult process, since it often results in a loss of control, choice and autonomy for the person involved. This process might be refused so that offers of support are declined and care needs denied as illustrated by the woman who refused to be cared for by her daughters: 'She was very naughty when her own daughters came. She wouldn't let them bath her, she'd keep throwing the soap out of the bath. And she was difficult if they tried to dress her' (Cotterill, 1994, p.163). Such behaviour suggests a determined effort to refuse the adoption of a new subject position as dependent and in need of care. However, for older people, the physical effects of ageing upon their bodies, together with the care needed to attend to those effects, can be very difficult to deny, which, in turn, can have a profound impact on their sense of themselves. The transgression of bodily boundaries that intimate physical care necessitates can also be profoundly unsettling (**Shildrick, 2004**). As Julia Twigg (2000, p.42) has argued, '[Some older people] seemed to undergo a total loss of self, going through a radical process of withdrawal and disengagement. It was not that they attempted to transcend their decaying bodies so much as that their very selfhood was annihilated, leaving just the empty body behind'.

Moreover, the crossing of another boundary by care workers – that of the 'public/private' divide – in order to deliver care services means that, for older people and disabled people alike, their home can no longer be regarded as an inviolable 'site of identity and self-expression, an opportunity to extend the self in material surroundings' (Twigg, 2000, p.78). Domestic space plays a central role in the construction, articulation and protection of what we understand to be our 'personal', for it often represents the most intimate and private aspects of our lives. When domestic space is breached because of care needs, this challenges the boundaries of our personal lives and leaves the making of our selves in that space permanently unsettled.

We can see then that care relationships and care activities provoke deep emotional and psychological responses, and influence how we understand who we are, the way we relate to others and what we understand to be our social and moral obligations to provide care. This is because, as Beverley Skeggs (1997, p.69) has argued, '"[t]he caring self" is both a performance and a technique used to generate valuations of responsibility and respectability'. This 'caring self' is not simply constructed relationally in the context of family, kin and friendship ties, despite the ways in which the gendered norms of femininity and motherhood – and indeed masculinity and fatherhood – contribute towards normalizing and naturalizing the social relations of care (Skeggs, 1997). The chapters in this book illustrate that it is not just care relations between close friends and family members that raise questions about our identities, but that all the spaces and places of care in which we are located can unsettle or validate the ways in which we claim or invoke our sense of self.

In Chapter 2, Holden demonstrates how care activities, as both paid and unpaid work, were central to the construction of single women's identities – as professional and nurturing individuals – and how these identities allowed them to further their own personal interests and aspirations in their 'public' and 'private' lives. However, the intersections of class, gender and ethnicity are also shown to have had intense significance to the ways in which single women were able to identify themselves as 'carers' and to the value that they placed on that identity. For example, the status, opportunities and rewards that care and service work offered to British middle-class women were arguably greater than those open to British working-class women who, in turn, had more choices in the employment market than Irish migrant women, of both the working and middle classes. This meant that different constituencies of single women constructed very different caring identities since their engagement with the relations and practices of care were structured by hierarchies of class, ethnicity, age and marital status, as well as by their different emotional commitments to their employment. At the same time, such hierarchies shaped women's engagement with the feminine norms of love, duty and reciprocity, and negotiations of expectations that they should care. Undoubtedly, some women did conform to normative expectations of themselves as gendered and 'racialized' welfare subjects, but others resisted or negotiated those expectations. Care relations were, therefore, central to constructing the boundaries of a gendered and racialized 'personal', but the nature of those relations – and by association 'the personal' – was always given meaning through its location in a particular time and place.

ACTIVITY 5.1

Reflect now on Chapter 3 by Barry Goldson and Chapter 4 by Yasmin Gunaratnam. How do ideas about gender (or femininities and masculinities) work in these chapters to:

■ shape the identities of different carers?

■ construct the different spaces of care addressed in the chapters?

How did these identities and spaces shape the processes of care in the different institutional locations? To what extent were other 'differences' influential in these contexts?

In Chapter 3, Barry Goldson highlights how the experiences of working in secure accommodation units can unsettle the identities of some staff as welfare professionals with a remit to 'care' for vulnerable children in their charge. Sometimes, the worries, questions and difficulties that evoke this unsettling are explicitly expressed as in, for example, the following quotation from Goldson's chapter by a member of staff in a secure unit: 'I worry about it all the time ... A question that I ask myself is that as an adult if I did the same behaviour would I be locked-up for my own good. In most cases I wouldn't. It's a question of rights and who has the right to decide what is best. It is really difficult' (Chapter 3, section 4.3.1).

Worrying 'all the time' illustrates the extent to which our personal lives are shaped by the nature of our work, whatever its formation (**Mooney, 2004**). Goldson illustrates that the imaginary boundary between the so-called 'masculine' public world and 'feminine' private world is profoundly challenged by both care relations in locked institutions and the notion of 'the personal'. We can see that there is no easy divide between the two worlds. Some staff are deeply troubled by their failure to translate the gendered values and norms of caring (that are traditionally associated with the 'private' sphere) into meaningful practices in the workplace. Similarly, we can appreciate the extent to which their 'personal' is constructed relationally through the engagement with the children in their charge, with other staff and with the rules and regulations imposed within the institutions. Goldson's interviews with staff illustrate how policy responses to the care and control of children perceived to be at risk to themselves or to others, and the development of institutional regimes to undertake that care and control, are crucial to their identities as welfare professionals and, in turn, to shaping their personal lives.

Being employed in institutions that are charged with the responsibility of delivering care to vulnerable children but which, at the same time, are widely acknowledged as having 'uncaring' regimes and practices is negotiated in two ways by staff whose professional identities are forged in this contested site of welfare/justice. Some staff, as the quotation above demonstrates, resist the rhetorical claims that legitimize such punitive interventions in some children's lives and, instead, articulate their concerns about not only the efficacy of the policy of securing children, but also the controlling aspects of the institutional regime. In this way staff can identify themselves primarily as caring individuals who seek to ameliorate, in whatever way possible, the experiences of children in secure accommodation. Moreover, this can also be a strategy to refuse or resist a wider group/professional identity and indeed agency imperatives. Such a strategy elides their involvement in the practices and effects placing children in secure units, at both policy and institutional level.

Other staff, however, defend their involvement in both these practices and the poor quality of care available to vulnerable children. They construct and invoke their identities as welfare professionals, and caring individuals, in this uneasy terrain by drawing upon policy discourses that emphasize the difficult personal lives of children in secure accommodation. Emphasis is placed, for example, on how secure accommodation 'keeps them safe', 'keeps them alive', because the children are all identified as 'at serious risk' and often with 'serious self-harm issues' (see Chapter 3, section 4.3.1). Defining the children in this way reinforces the identities of staff as caring welfare professionals since they construct themselves as acting in the best interests of their charges whose personal lives are seen as needing control, regulation or protection. As a result, the staff are able to make clear distinctions between their own personal lives, which are not subject to similar interventions, and the lives of children they encounter in institutional settings.

A concern with the relationship between personal lives, care relations and the construction of identities is also evident in Chapter 4. Here, Gunaratnam queries the 'natural' categories of identity that individuals are understood to be born into and argues that we should reject assumptions about the meanings of, for example, 'race' and ethnicity. Rather, she insists that we should ask how particular categories are given meaning, by whom and when. This means that as we read the hospice accounts within the chapter, we should not assume what it means, for example, to be a 'Ugandan woman with AIDS, or a white, English woman hospice nurse' (Chapter 4, section 2.1), nor should we presume to know what it means to be 'Ugandan' or a 'nurse'. Gunaratnam argues that we need to consider how categories of identity are given meaning, how their boundaries are constructed and maintained and, also, to question the relationships between different categories of identity and the social effects of them.

Using psychoanalytic tools, Gunaratnam points to the unconscious and conscious processes through which the nurses that she interviewed constructed themselves as white professionals. In particular, her analysis of the interview extracts teases out their emotions and unconscious anxieties. The hospice nurses interviewed by Gunaratnam, like the secure unit staff discussed above, demonstrate the ways in which care relations and practices can simultaneously construct and undermine both a professional identity and an identity as a caring individual. In the case of Gill and Roz, this process emerges through their prevarications in the interview, and the doubts and difficulties that they express as the following brief excerpts from Chapter 4 illustrate:

Gill Yes. Yeah. I'm trying to think of the right word, but yes that's what I
       mean ... So it was very difficult, but I found we never really got alongside
       her ... I suppose I view that as a failure of care in a way ... So you know I
       don't know really (laughs).

       ...

Roz I think it's a feeling that you might have failed them ... that for me is quite
       hard, cause I think 'well, as a nurse I'm here cause I want to be useful' ...
       So is that me having a problem because I haven't achieved, cause I want
       the sort of kick I want to get out of nursing?

(Chapter 4, section 4)

The evidence from qualitative data such as interviews and personal narratives
are thus able to highlight the speaker's subjectivity and point to their
individual agency. They are, therefore, valuable resources both to explore the
presentation of the self and to understand how the individual self is
constructed and maintained (Chamberlayne et al., 2000).

Using the different tools of psychoanalytic, feminist, social constructionist and
postcolonial theory, the chapters in this book have foregrounded the complex
processes through which caring identities are produced. Welfare practitioners
and family carers are shown to struggle in the construction of themselves as
caring subjects at all times, and in all spaces and places of care. These selves
are constructed through the material and historical contexts of care but, in
particular, through the physical, emotional and psychic dynamics of the care
encounter. Caring and professional identities are, therefore, always in flux and
always unstable. This can mean that, just as those receiving care accept,
negotiate or challenge the services that they are offered, so the personal
contexts of welfare professionals' lives are crucial to their manipulation (for
good or ill) of the discourses, policies and practices that define and construct
their encounters with service users. One key element in the mutual
constitution of personal lives and social policy can thus be traced in these
relational processes through which the identities of service users and welfare
practitioners are experienced and given meaning.

4   Morality

The meanings and identities that we have traced through the analysis of care
relations and practices across the different chapters draw upon wider and
deeper questions about society's moral norms, expectations and values. You
may have noticed references in the chapters to, for example, 'moral
responsibility', 'moral authority' and 'moral duty'. We might argue that one of
the reasons for such references is that care is often regarded as a site of
'natural' morality – like that of 'the family'. The provision of care and family
life are both understood to involve relationships in which love, trust, nurture
and support are 'naturally' and 'normally' clustered. Indeed, the normative
assumptions that are associated with the domains of care and 'the family'

should not be surprising given that, as we noted above, they have become
bracketed together in both social policy and the social sciences more
generally. However, such an emphasis on the relationship between care and
'natural' morality means that particular forms of care relations – such as those
between mother and child – become idealized, and it is difficult to recognize
other practices, activities and meanings (Davidoff et al., 1999). At the same
time, this idealization of care makes recognition of the workings of power,
control or aggression that are present at some point in all care relationships –
not just pathological ones – impossible to acknowledge. One of the aims of
this book has been, therefore, to unsettle such idealizations and to point to the
diversity and plurality in the forms and practices of care.

We can see from each of the chapters the ways in which individuals draw
upon moral norms and values to explain their actions, rationalize their
behaviour and interpret their emotions. For example, the interview with Gill
and Roz, which forms such a key element of Chapter 4, illustrates both the
significance that they give to their professional status as nurses and carers but,
at the same time, the moral dilemmas that such a status brings. Running
throughout the interview is a sense that they had failed – not just at a
professional level but also at a moral one – to fulfil their responsibilities to the
Ugandan woman whom they had nursed. As we argued above, this perceived
failure unsettled their professional and caring identities, but their ambivalent
recognition of this failure also demonstrates the deep-seated norms and values
that we attach to care relations, how we seek to negotiate them, and how
issues of 'race' and ethnicity as well as gender are drawn into those
negotiations.

Such issues are clear, too, in the example of women missionaries (discussed in
Chapter 2) who deployed hierarchies of class, gender and ethnicity to
construct their white, maternal, Christian identities, which enabled them to
assert and justify their moral authority over the women and children to whom
they offered care and education. Such claims to moral authority were also
used by welfare professionals in this same period to justify their interventions
in the lives of young women who were understood to be sexually immoral or
morally vulnerable and, therefore, in need of regulation or protection by the
state and its agencies.

The constitution of some children, families and groups of individuals as in
need of moral reclamation or moral control is also evident in Goldson's
discussion of the ways in which welfare/justice interventions in the lives of
children seen to be 'at risk' or as posing 'a risk to others' are justified. Chapter
3 alerts us to how the state's moralistic gaze has tended to focus upon the lives
of disadvantaged children and families through notions of (ir)responsibility,
(im)morality and (in)discipline, while the material conditions of poverty and
inequality of their lives are largely neglected. As Goldson argues, this gaze is
largely class specific, but it is also gendered and racialized. Historically,
therefore, the criminal behaviour of working-class boys and girls is judged by
gendered criteria with girls being held in institutions for the care and control
of children because of their 'sexual delinquency' and 'sexual immorality'. 'In
other words, overtly gendered constructions of sexuality and adolescent

behaviour can serve to precipitate the restriction of liberty in respect of girls in ways that do not normally apply to boys' (Chapter 3, section 4.2).

Running across the book as a whole then, we can appreciate the extent to which notions of morality are significant to the construction and validation of caring identities, but that we negotiate what is understood to be 'right' in the specific contexts of our care relations. As Irwin and Williams (2002, p.4) have argued, this helps us see that '... the study of morality/values is not simply about abstract principles, as articulated through religion, philosophy or law, but is something that is worked out in concrete situations and, importantly, in relationships with others'.

But, we can also begin to understand how particular moral norms and values are embedded in social policy, and the ways in which they inform the practices and discourses of welfare professionals. There is an expectation that people *should* behave in a certain way – as parents (**Doolittle, 2004**; **Lucey, 2004**), as young people (**Thomson, 2004**), as disabled people (**Shildrick, 2004**), as workers (**Mooney, 2004**) or as citizens (**Lewis, 2004**) – and this behaviour is judged, measured and regulated through welfare practice, social policy and the law. In the context of care, it is by transgressing moral expectations and refusing our moral responsibilities, both of which for the purposes of the law and social policy are constituted in the 'public' realm, that our personal lives become the subject of intervention by the state. Private conceptions of what is right and their shaping of 'the personal' are negotiated through, and in opposition to, wider social and political norms and values, and in conjunction with, for example, counter discourses offered by family and alternative value systems or habits of everyday life.

5   Conclusion

Our emphasis on the practices, relations and meanings of care has been driven by a determination to illustrate the role that care plays in the mutual constitution of personal lives and social policy. We have rejected common assumptions that relationships of care between individuals are located in the most private and intimate sphere of our personal lives, and that our ways of understanding ourselves as carers or recipients of care are based on private norms, values and attitudes. Care and caring – those seemingly most 'personal' of activities, emotions and feelings – are shown, through the chapters of this book, to be interpreted and constituted through the particular social meanings, interactions and contexts of care. In this, social policy and the practices of welfare professionals are crucial to the legitimization, surveillance and control of care practices in both the 'public' and 'private' spheres, and thereby to the shaping of personal lives.

However, we have also demonstrated that individuals do not always readily accept, identify with or respond to particular norms of care that have been validated in welfare knowledges and implemented through particular welfare practices. Neither do they easily accept the normalized and normalizing obligations and responsibilities of care that are embedded in familial relationships. The interactions between welfare professionals and their clients illustrate the feelings of ambivalence and unease that practices and relations of care can provoke in institutional settings. Similar feelings are readily identifiable in domestic sites of care. The troubling dimensions of these interactions can be productive for they open up opportunities for individuals to consider different ways of caring for and about each other that challenge normative assumptions, acceptable behaviours and appropriate practices in both the 'public' and 'private' domains.

Care relations can be seen, then, as an influential channel through which personal lives are shaped by the interventions of social policy and welfare practices, but which, at the same time, challenge the imperatives and assumptions of policy-making. The analytic lens of care thus throws much valuable light on the complex ways in which personal lives and social policy are mutually constituted.

References

Carabine, J. (ed.) (2004) *Sexualities: Personal Lives and Social Policy*, Bristol, The Policy Press in association with The Open University.

Chamberlayne, P., Bornat, J. and Wengraf, T. (2000) 'Introduction: the biographical turn' in Chamberlayne, P., Bornat, J. and Wengraf, T. (eds) *The Turn to Biographical Methods in Social Science: Comparative Issues and Examples*, London, Routledge.

Cotterill, P. (1994) *Friendly Relations? Mothers and their Daughters-in-Law*, London, Taylor and Francis.

Davidoff, L., Doolittle, M., Fink, J. and Holden, K. (1999) *The Family Story: Blood, Contract and Intimacy 1830–1960*, London, Longman.

Doolittle, M. (2004) 'Sexuality, parenthood and population: explaining fertility decline in Britain from the 1860s to 1920s' in Carabine (ed.) (2004).

Forster, M. (1981) *Mother Can You Hear Me?*, Harmondsworth, Penguin.

Irwin, S. and Williams, F. (2002) 'Understanding social values and social change: the case of care, family and intimacy', Paper presented at the ESPRN conference on Social Values and Social Policies, Netherlands, University of Tilburg.

Lewis, G. (ed.) (2004) *Citizenship: Personal Lives and Social Policy*, Bristol, The Policy Press in association with The Open University.

Lucey, H. (2004) 'Differentiated citizenship: psychic defence, social division and the construction of local secondary school markets' in Lewis (ed.) (2004).

Mooney, G. (ed.) (2004) *Work: Personal Lives and Social Policy*, Bristol, The Policy Press in association with The Open University.

Morgan, D. (1996) *Family Connections*, Cambridge, Polity Press.

Shildrick, M. (2004) 'Silencing sexuality: the regulation of the disabled body' in Carabine (ed.) (2004).

Skeggs, B. (1997) *Formations of Class and Gender*, London, Sage.

Thomson, R. (2004) 'Sexuality and young people: policies, practices and identities' in Carabine (ed.) (2004).

Twigg, J. (2000) *Bathing – The Body and Community Care*, London, Routledge.

Acknowledgements

Grateful acknowledgement is made to the following sources for permission to reproduce material within this book:

Figures/Illustrations

Figure 1.1: right: Copyright © British Red Cross; *Figure 1.3: left:* Copyright © John Birdsall Photography; *Figure 1.3: right:* Copyright © John Birdsall Photography; *Figure 1.5:* Copyright © James Robertson; *Figure 1.6: Guardian Society*, 12 February 2003. Copyright © Hector Breeze; *Figure 1.7: left:* Copyright © Judy Harrison / Photofusion; *Figure 1.7: right:* Copyright © John Birdsall Photography; *Figure 2.1:* from: Mary S. Allen, *The Pioneer Policewoman*, London, Chatto & Windus, 1925; *Figure 2.2:* from: *Woman's Friend*, 15 January 1938; *Figure 2.3:* from: Mary Heath-Stubbs, *Friendships Highway: Being the History of the Girls' Friendly Society, 1875–1935*, London, GFS Central Office, 1935; *Figure 2.4(a):* from: *Good Housekeeping*, April 1933; *Figure 2.4(b):* from: *Good Housekeeping*, April 1933; *Figure 2.5:* from: Phyllis Willmott, *A Singular Woman: The Life of Geraldine Aves, 1898–1986*, London, Whiting & Birch Ltd, 1992; *Figure 2.6:* Copyright © West Yorkshire Archive Service. www.archives.wyjs.org.uk; *Figure 2.7:* Copyright © Katherine Holden; *Figure 3.3:* Copyright © National Archives; *Figure 3.5:* Copyright © ID.8 Photography; *Figure 4.1:* Copyright © Science Photo Library; *Figure 4.2:* 'Be part of the new NHS'. Crown copyright material is reproduced under Class Licence Number C01W0000065 with the permission of the Controller of HMSO and the Queen's Printer for Scotland; *Figure 4.3:* Copyright © Willi & Deni McIntyre / Science Photo Library; *Figure 4.4:* Copyright © Graham Maxwell; *Figure 4.5:* Copyright © Gisele Wulfsohn / Panos Pictures; *Figure 4.6:* Copyright © *New Internationalist*, vol.346, June 2002. www.newint.org.

Every effort has been made to contact copyright holders. If any have been inadvertently overlooked, the publishers will be pleased to make the necessary arrangements at the first opportunity.

Index

Girls' Friendly Society (GFS) 52–3
Gittens, Diana 73
global care chain 17
Goldson, B. 107
Good Housekeeping
    cartoons on domestic service
      56–7
    'Four in family' 69–70
Graham, Eleanor, *The Children
    who Lived in a Barn* 48
Graham, Hilary 6, 27, 28, 64
Green, J. 122
Griffiths Report (1988) 31
Gunaratnam, Yasmin 18, 141

Hall, Stuart 48
Harris, R. 107
health care, and the provision of
    social care 33–4
Heath-Stubbs, M. 52–3
Hendrick, H. 107
heterosexuality, and the provision
    of care 3
Hochschild, Arlie 17, 29, 51
Hodgkin, Rachel 96
Holden family in inter-war Britain
    70–1
Holden, Katherine 73–4
holistic care, in hospices 117, 118,
    137
hospices
    AIDS patients
      Kenyan man 134–6
      Ugandan woman 112,
        123–8, 129–30, 132,
        134, 136, 137, 138–9
    and holistic care 117, 118, 137
    and intercultural care 4, 8, 18,
      112, 114, 117–23
    dietary requirements 119,
      139
    and difference 117–19
    and ethnic minority staff
      119
    identities in caring
      relationships 153–4
    individual accounts of
      117, 123–8, 129–30,
      131–2, 136–7, 137–
      40, 153–4, 155
    nurse education and
      training in cultural
      competence 119–23
    and postcolonialism 137–
      40

religious requirements 119
and the voluntary sector 117
hospitals
    children in 19–20
    nurses and unconscious
      anxieties 21
Hudson, Annie 96
human rights, and children in
    locked institutions 96, 100, 101
Humphries, Stephen 92

idealization, and splitting 68
identifying carers 8–12
identities in caring relationships
    37, 147, 150–4
    and the care and control of
      children 152–3
    carers 32, 150
    and class 151
    different categories of and
      health care 115
    and gender 151–2
    older people and loss of self
      150–1
    and 'race' 151–2, 153–4
    unmarried women in inter-
      war Britain 151–2
independence, and care relations
    14, 36, 37
independent living movement 13,
    14
industrial schools, and nineteenth-
    century children 88, 90
inequalities
    and disadvantaged children
      79, 81–2
    and the nineteenth-
      century institutional
      'fix' 90
    postcolonial 140
    and poverty in the UK 93, 105
    in the treatment of AIDS/HIV
      138, 139
informal care 5, 8
    and lack of financial reward
      34–5
    and principles of reciprocity
      and redistribution 33
    and social policy 34–5
    see also carers
institutional care
    older people in 35–6
      in the inter-war years
        62–3
    and unconscious anxieties 21

and women as paid care
    workers 15
institutional care for children 4, 79,
    86, 94–05
    controversy and paradox in
      94–8
    and disadvantage 97–8
    locked institutions 91, 92, 93,
      94–105, 106
    in the nineteenth century 87–
      92
    and personal lives 98–105
    and psychoanalytic theory
      19–20
    staff 98–9
      and identities in caring
        relationships 152–3
      in secure accommodation
        units 99–100, 101
      in young offender
        institutions 102–4
    see also secure
      accommodation; young
      offender institutions
institutional racism
    and the care and control of
      children 81, 82, 97
    and intercultural hospice care
      in the health services 112
inter-generational differentiation,
    and social constructions of
    childhood 81, 87
intercultural communicative
    competence, nurse education
    and training in 121
intimate relationships and care 7,
    15
    same-sex relationships 28
intra-generational differentiation,
    and the social construction of
    childhood 81, 82
Irish migrant women, in domestic
    service 58–9, 60, 151
Irwin, S. 156

Jamieson, Lynn, *Intimacy* 37
Jenks, Chris 78
Johnson, Julia 8
Jones, C. 107

Keith, Lois 28–9
Kelly, B. 107
Kestenbaum, A. 14
Kim, Y.Y. 121
Klein, Melanie 67, 71